COPING WITH THE DISRUPTIVE COLLEGE STUDENT:
A Practical Model

By Gerald Amada, Ph.D

Michael Clay Smith, J.D., Ed.D., LL.M., Legal Consultant

The Higher Education Administration Series
Edited by Donald D. Gehring and D. Parker Young

COLLEGE ADMINISTRATION PUBLICATIONS, INC.

College Administration Publications, Inc.,
P. O. Box 15898, Asheville, NC 28813-0898

©1994 College Administration Publications, Inc.,
All rights reserved. Published 1994
Printed in the United States of America

Library of Congress Cataloging-in-Publication Data

Amada, Gerald
    Coping with the disruptive college student : a practical model /
by Gerald Amada : legal consultant, Michael Clay Smith.
      p.   cm. — (The Higher education administration series)
    Includes bibliographical references.
    ISBN 0-912557-16-8 : $14.95
    1. College discipline—United States. 2. Counseling in higher
education—United States. I. Smith, Michael Clay. II. Title.
III. Series.
LB2344.A48   1993
378.1'8'0973—dc20   93-34165
                                                                                           CIP

    Brief quotation may be used in critical articles or reviews. For any other reproduction of the book, however, including electronic, mechanical, photocopying, recording or other means, written permission must be obtained from the publisher.
    The views expressed in this book are those of the individual authors and are not necessarily those of College Administration Publications, Inc.
    This publication is designed to provide accurate and authoritative information in regard to the subject matter covered. It is sold with the understanding that the publisher is not engaged in rendering legal, accounting or other professional service. If legal advice or other expert assistance is required, the services of a competent professional person should be sought.
        —*from a Declaration of Principles jointly adopted by a committee of the American Bar Association and a committee of publishers.*

This book is dedicated to my grandchildren, who are, chronologically and belovedly,

Rachel Tzucker
Rebecca Tzucker
Jordan Ehrlich
Matthew Ehrlich
Joshua Tzucker

Table of Contents

Foreword • *vii*

Preface • *ix*

About the Author • *xi*

About the Legal Consultant • *xiii*

I. **Introduction** • 1

II. **A Code of Student Conduct** • 7
    A Definition of Disruption • 8
    Five Principles • 11
    Disciplinary Sanctions • 14

III. **Recommended Procedures for Dealing With Incidents of Disruptions** • 17
    Essential Prerogatives • 18
    Documentation • 19
    Non-Instructional Staff • 20
    The Aversion to Administering Discipline • 21
    The Special Burdens Carried by Administrators • 22
    An Institutional Anomaly • 26
    A Few Alternatives • 28
        Waiting For Sufficient Grounds • 28
        Filing Criminal Charges • 28
        Taking Legal Action Against One's Own College • 29

IV. **Due Process for the Disruptive Student** • 31
    Sanctions • 34
    Disclosure • 35

V. **Disruptiveness in Residence Halls** • 39
  Dealing With Harassment of Residential Staff • 42
    Countermeasures to Harassment • 42
  Dealing With the Problem of Rape • 43
  Coping With Self-Destructive Students • 44
  Assaults, Thefts, and Vandalism • 46
  Dealing With Various Forms of Harassment • 47

VI. **The Role of the College Mental Health Program** • 51
  The Increasing Number of Disruptive College Students • 51
  Mandatory Psychotherapy as a Form of Discipline • 53
    Requiring Disruptive Students To
      Receive Psychotherapy • 53
    Motivations for Requiring Psychotherapy • 54
    Required Psychotherapy as a Coercive Measure • 55
    Confidentiality in Psychotherapy • 55
    Required Psychotherapy as a Transfer of Authority • 56
    Required Psychotherapy and Section 504 • 56
  The Role of the Mental Health Consultant • 58
    A Discussion Regarding a Disruptive Student • 58

VII. **Some Special Problems** • 65
  Disruptiveness Versus Dangerousness • 65
  Mental Illness and Dangerousness • 66
  The Use of Mandatory Psychiatric Withdrawals • 67
  Conditions of Re-Enrollment • 72
  Conflicts Over the Use of Medications • 73
  The Disruptive Non-Student • 74
  Child Care • 75
  A Restroom Problem • 77
  Coping With Epithetic Language or
    Socially Offensive Dress • 78

VIII. **Case Studies** • 81
  I. You Can't Tell Me Where To Go! • 81
  II. Let Me Show You My Etchings! • 86
  III. Me and My Shadow • 95
  IV. Disruptive, Disruptive ... *Who's* Disruptive? • 101
  V. An Example of Reasonable Accommodation • 105

Bibliography • 109

Foreword

Those of us who have dealt with students on a daily basis over a period of years have come to realize that there are increasing numbers of disruptive students on campus today. Their disruptive activity takes many forms. Sometimes they violate specific sections of our code of conduct, but other times their behavior is simply obnoxious or a manifestation of incivility.

Many college administrators, especially those in student affairs, are very tolerant of those who act "differently." Thus, students who do not cross the line of violating campus rules, but who make life difficult for others, frustrate college officials who are befuddled when it comes to responding to such individuals. There are also students who do cross the line and violate campus rules and regulations, disrupting the normal campus environment. However, administrators see more than a discipline problem in the behavior of these disruptive individuals. The students' behavior may have been precipitated by a dysfunctional family life, substance abuse, or the influence of violence in film or on TV. To simply discipline such individuals will not solve the problem. What do you do?

In this publication Dr. Amada offers several alternatives for responding to "disruptive students" whether they be those who make life difficult for others or those who actually violate campus codes for whatever reason. He writes from the perspective of a mental health professional with years of experience. He provides reasonable and tested methods and presents them clearly without the use of jargon. His writing is not legalistic, but his suggestions are within the parameters of the law.

The disruptive individual is a problem which must be faced and this is a book whose time has come.

—Donald D. Gehring, *Series Editor*

Preface

The principles, recommendations and perspectives contained in the following chapters are to a large extent the outgrowth of discussions and consultations I have had with a vast number of colleagues, both at my own college, City College of San Francisco, and at numerous other campuses throughout the United States and Canada. I wish to thank these individuals collectively for raising crucial questions and proffering insightful advice regarding the issue of the disruptive college student. Their contribution has been to stretch and refine my thinking on this complicated subject, for which I am enormously grateful. I sincerely hope they will accept my apology for not being mentioned by name, but their sheer numbers made this an unfortunate impossibility.

My legal sidekick on this project, Dr. Michael Clay Smith, deserves special thanks for his generous and assiduous assistance throughout our collaboration. It eased my mind immeasurably to know that, despite his very hectic professional schedule, Mike would always be unstintingly "there" and ready to help.

I owe a special debt of gratitude to Dr. Donald D. Gehring and Mr. George J. Searle, Jr., Co-Editor and General Manager, respectively, of College Administration Publications, Inc., for the care and dedication with which they helped to shepherd this project to its final publication.

I also wish to thank my children, Robin, Naomi, Laurie and Eric, and my sons-in-law, Jay and Scott, for the unfaltering understanding and affection with which they have nurtured me. However, this book probably would not have been written were it not for the abiding love and help given to me by my wife, Marcia. It was her gentle but inspirational goading, in the form of occasional comments such as, "Jerry, you obviously know this subject pretty well, so why don't you write a book about it," that dissolved some stymieing mental logjam and allowed me to push ahead with this publication. For that, and much more, I owe Marcia my deepest love, respect and appreciation.

Finally, this book is dedicated to my grandchildren. They, and their compeers around the world, are the newfledged torchbearers of dreams and hopes for a better world. It is my profoundest wish that they carry their torches high, with dignity, moral courage, and compassionate regard for the welfare of others and themselves.

About the Author

Dr. Gerald Amada is the Co-Director and one of the founders of the City College of San Francisco Mental Health Program. He is the author of several books, including *A Guide to Psychotherapy*, which will be republished by Ballantine Books (Random House) in 1994. In addition, he has published over thirty articles and reviews on the subjects of mental health and psychotherapy. Dr. Amada has also been a book and manuscript reviewer for the *American Journal of Psychotherapy*, University Press of America, the *Journal of College Student Psychotherapy*, and the San Francisco *Chronicle*.

He is the recipient of the 1984 Award of Excellence in the category of Administrator, Post Secondary Education, conferred by the National Association of Vocational Education Special Needs Personnel, Region V (comprising eighteen states).

Dr. Amada wishes to express his thanks and appreciation to the *Journal of American College Health*, Helen Dwight Reid Educational Foundation, for allowing him permission to reprint major portions of two articles that he published in that journal: "Dealing with the Disruptive College Student: Some Theoretical and Practical Considerations"; 1986; 34:221-225 and "Coping with the Disruptive College Student: A Practical Model;" 1992; 40:203-215, Heldref Publications, 1319 18th Street, N.W., Washington, D.C., 20036-1802. Copyright 1986 and 1992, respectively.

About the Legal Consultant

Dr. Michael Clay Smith is Professor of Criminal Justice and Education Administration at The University of Southern Mississippi.

His background includes many years of experience as an administrator and attorney for institutions of higher education.

He is author of three books, including Coping with Crime on Campus (Macmillan, 1988), and more than thirty articles in legal, education and criminology journals. He holds degrees in law from Tulane Law School and Mississippi College, and a doctorate in higher education administration from West Virginia University.

Chapter I

Introduction

Traditionally regarded as safe and hospitable havens for young students, the typical contemporary college no longer stands apart from the stresses and violent social upheavals that take place in the society outside its hallowed walls. College officials observe with increasing alarm that today's students are becoming increasingly disrespectful of institutional authority, flagrant in their willingness to flout college rules and regulations and, in some instances, behave quite menacingly toward college staff in an attempt to gratify their own wishes and demands.

Although there are no reliable statistics with which to assess the dimensions of this problem on a national scale, it is now evident that disruptive and even violent behavior on the nation's college campuses has become legion. Common forms of student misconduct include cheating, verbal abuse, physical threats, property damage, alcohol and drug abuse, and, in extreme cases, acts of violence (including murder).

Students who take umbrage with their instructors over a low grade may stalk and threaten them in an attempt to redress their grievance. It is not uncommon for some students to form close and erotic attachments to professors and teaching assistants and then shadow them or pursue them with persistent phone calls or letters. Perhaps the most common form of disruptive behavior in the classroom (aside from cheating) is the hectoring and badgering that some students use to interrupt lectures and humiliate instructors in order to gain attention and notoriety.

According to one college official, "We are seeing more aberrant and seriously disruptive behavior on campus. And I'm persuaded that there are more people with problems out there who need the help of the institution. It has to do with dysfunctional families, the upwardly mobile pressures of the last decade, stress from the academic program and the impact of substance abuse on a wide scale." (Carmody, 1990, Section B, p. 7)

Whatever its causes, there is clear unanimity among college and university administrators that the problem of student disruptiveness has already reached alarming proportions and therefore requires a thorough review of college judicial and disciplinary procedures in order to maximize their effectiveness in dealing with student misconduct. As well, college officials are also developing crisis intervention teams with which to intervene in cases of campus disruption and violence. In order accurately to document and monitor incidents of disruptiveness some colleges are now creating a central registry of incident reports.

Although we have witnessed in recent years a dramatic rise in the number of serious incidents of disruption on college campuses, disruption and violence are hardly new phenomena in academia. As far back as 1354 enmity between the scholars of Oxford University and the townsfolk of the surrounding community erupted into bloody violence. In the wake of this rampage the university was pillaged and many were killed, including two chaplains who were flayed alive (Schachner, 1938). Over five centuries later, at this same prestigious university, Oscar Wilde was physically assaulted by his academic compeers perhaps for no other reason than that he was deemed by them to be a dandiacal show-off. College records of the time also indicate that a substantial number of Oxonians were punished with rustication for failure to pay their tuition debts (Ellman, 1988).

In the first half of the nineteenth century, many college students rebelled, often violently, against the harsh discipline and austere living conditions of the university. Between 1820 and 1840, there were many riots at the University of Virginia, one of which resulted in the killing of a professor. Earlier in that century, in 1807, a riot at Princeton University led to the suspension of half the student body. A few years later, Princeton students attempted to burn several campus outbuildings (Brubacher and Rudy, 1976).

In 1841, at another elite institution, Yale University, students overcame firefighters in the street and destroyed their equipment. Several years later a bartender was killed in a clash between Yale students and townsfolk, and, four years later, a student shot and killed a firefighter in the second "Fireman's Riot." Also in the early part of the nineteenth century, Harvard University was beset by unrest and brawls that caused a student to lose his eye and, on another occasion, the suspension of more than half of the senior class on the eve of commencement (Brubacher and Rudy, 1976).

Although there were sporadic incidents of disruption, sometimes with tragic consequences, on the college campuses of the nineteenth century, the frequency and seriousness of those incidents have been completely eclipsed by the recurrent and sometimes virulent forms of student misconduct that are beleaguering many of our contemporary colleges and universities. What social forces have precipitated and propelled this trend toward untamed and indiscriminate disruptiveness?

As pointed out by the above-quoted college administrator, there are, more than ever before, large numbers of emotionally troubled students from dysfunctional families attending college and behaving disruptively. To complicate matters, the national recession that has produced widespread unemployment and financial instability in millions of households throughout the country, has certainly taken its toll upon college students. Many students can financially sustain themselves only if they hold a job while attending college. Many choose a sequence of academic courses and a career, not necessarily according to their wishes, goals or aptitudes, but primarily according to practical considerations that they and their parents deem sensible in today's shrinking job market. Many college students, when they look toward the future, see bleak economic prospects awaiting them. Given their fears and doubts about their future employability, it is not surprising that a great many students become obsessed with attaining high grades, develop a fierce and unhealthy sense of competition toward their academic peers, and even resort to cheating as a means of getting ahead through "beating the system."

For a great many students, economic privation has also adversely affected the quality of family life. Because many students cannot afford to attend college on a full-time basis, their college years become protracted. Consequently, they may reside at home with their parents and siblings well into their adulthood, living in a state of indefinite and unwanted financial and emotional dependency. To the young student who aspires, above all else, to achieve age-appropriate independence and individuality, this extended period of dependency upon family can disrupt these all-important developmental strivings.

The ubiquity of drugs and the regular exposure of most persons, including students, to wanton violence in the media are undoubtedly major, if indirect, contributors to various acts of disruptiveness on the college campus. A less obvious source of campus disruptiveness is the unique culture of the college environment itself. Generally, colleges offer an inimitably rich opportunity to students that splendidly fosters their personal growth and intellectual enlightenment. However, for many students, the college environment is experienced as harsh, fraught with great personal risks, and basically uncaring and insensitive to their needs. If this dim personal perspective is supported and validated by a college that lacks the programs, services or educational commitment to help the especially troubled student, there is increased likelihood that the troubled student will eventually become a disruptive student. Unless colleges carefully evaluate how well their programs and curricula are accommodating especially vulnerable students, a given student's disruptiveness will be narrowly viewed solely as a manifestation of his troubled personality or illness. Although this self-serving viewpoint may give comfort to those who must make judicial decisions regarding the disruptive student's behavior, it clearly does not serve either the student or the college especially well. Obviously, it is in the college's interest to determine if there are particular sources of excessive stress that exist within the college community itself and, if possible, seek to remedy or at least ameliorate these sources of trouble. Of course, some disruptive students will continue to behave disruptively in even the most idyllic educational milieus. Others, however, respond well when their special educational and psychological needs are met on a timely basis.

Most colleges and universities are struggling mightily to develop suitable programs for problematic students. Apparently, a majority of the nation's colleges are still in the process of developing and refining their codes of student conduct and judicial procedures in order to ensure that they are legally sound and enforceable. Yet, many if not most colleges still find themselves embattled and disarmed by disruptive students because of a lack of clarity regarding the college's legal rights and prerogatives vis-a-vis students who behave disruptively. Why are so many colleges finding it inordinately difficult to cope effectively with students who disrupt campus life?

Perhaps the answer lies, in part, in an understanding of the evolving history of educational institutions in this country. For a great many years, institutions of higher education empowered themselves with the right to control and govern the lives of students according to the common-law principle of *in loco parentis,* under which educational authorities assumed the role and authority of a student's parents. In many cases, college officials, operating under the principle of *in loco parentis,* arbitrarily assumed the power to regulate and legislate most aspects of a student's life, including one's moral attitudes and sexual behavior. One example of how colleges attempted to regulate and govern student behavior were the stringent curfews and surveillance that were imposed on students primarily, evidently, to desexualize their extracurricular goings-on. Clearly, when retrospectively judged by the less Puritanical standards and policies of most colleges in the 1990s, many of these moralistic practices could be justifiably characterized as rather heavy-handed and authoritarian.

In the 1960s the civil rights movement catalyzed the transformation of the nation's colleges and universities. College officials, beleaguered by thousands of demonstrating students, were forced to re-evaluate the appropriateness and legitimacy of their academic programs and administrative policies. Some college officials, cowed and bewildered by the onslaught of angry and sometimes violent students, reacted with indignation, rage and punitive sanctions. Others, not necessarily out of choice, reacted by relinquishing many of the long-held and long-cherished prerogatives that had formerly been used to control and discipline students.

The 1970s ushered into campus life a second round of mass protest, the Vietnam War demonstrations. Sit-ins, marches, draft-card burnings, and riots broke out on college campuses across the nation. Some of these demonstrations reached violent proportions, with lethal and tragic consequences, such as occurred at Kent State University when the National Guard fired into a crowd of students, killing four and wounding nine (Smith, 1989).

In the wake of these social upheavals, college and university administrators perforce sought to develop new and more enlightened administrative guidelines and policies for dealing with campus disruptions. Obviously, at most colleges, the pendulum of institutional authority has swung quite far away from the rigid enforcement of the outmoded principle of *in loco parentis;* not necessarily to the extreme of adopting a stance of absolute nonpaternalism or laissez-faireism, but more toward establishing judicial systems and educational services that are in concert with the legal standards and social mores of a radically changed society. Higher education institutions are now faced with the momentous challenge of how to replace effete and antiquated administrative methods of dealing with campus disruption with more humane, efficacious and legally sound practices. It is hoped that the practical model that is presented in the following chapters will help to fulfill that vital objective.

Chapter II

A Code of Student Conduct

As obvious and simplistic as this recommendation may seem, it is imperative to point out that colleges should periodically review their codes of student conduct for the following: Are the codes clear, coherent, comprehensive, mutually compatible and enforceable? Will they withstand legal scrutiny and challenge?

In a random survey of about twelve community colleges in California, I found, under the section dealing with student conduct in the college catalogs, that eight schools had rather clear and explicit codes of student conduct, three had vague, ambiguous references to the need for general conformity to the social and moral standards of the campus community, and, astonishingly, that one college had no written statement at all regarding student conduct. Clearly, this latter college unnecessarily places itself in potential legal jeopardy.

In reviewing the comprehensiveness of their student conduct codes, colleges should attempt to determine whether the codes will cover those forms of disruptive behavior that will arise most often on their campuses. Because obvious forms of disruptive behavior (i.e., conduct that is physically violent or overtly menacing)—are likely to be readily identified and included in the student conduct codes, colleges should also take heed to acknowledge in the codes, at least implicitly, that certain forms of passive and covert behavior may also be regarded as quite disruptive. These behaviors, although perhaps less frightening than violent actions, may be equally disruptive of the academic process.

Examples of passive, yet disruptive, behavior are those students whose poor personal hygiene so seriously offends the sensibilities of classmates and instructors that the classroom becomes an academic environment that is no longer tenable. It is not uncommon for instructors and other college staff to be deeply upset and offended by students who, week after week, carry with them to classes or administrative offices a foul bodily stench. In some instances, these students may be attending class immediately after a vigorous physical workout on the ball field, and therefore have not had an opportunity to shower. In other instances, the student is apparently a seriously psychologically disturbed individual, possibly living in a squalid and unhygienic home environment, who is altogether oblivious to his own bodily odors and the offensive effect they are having upon others. In several cases of this kind that have been reported to me by faculty at various colleges there was an actual danger that the class would be cancelled due to the anticipated attrition of students who were seriously considering dropping out to escape the revolting fetidity.

Another example of passive behavior that can be highly disruptive is the student who each day conspicuously falls asleep in a class in which oral participation is a clearly established academic requirement. Unquestionably, some of these students are persons who may be working long hours at a laborious job or taking care of small children until late into the night. Others, according to many staff reports, are persons with serious psychological disabilities such as schizophrenia. Their drowsiness may be one of the side-effects of their antipsychotic medications. Whatever their cause, however, certain passive but highly disruptive behaviors are quite common on college campuses and therefore probably deserve a place in the roster of behaviors that are proscribed by the college's code of student conduct.

To determine accurately the fairness, comprehensibility, and applicability of its codes of student conduct, administrators responsible for formulating and ultimately enforcing the codes should review them regularly with the administrative, instructional, and classified (support) staff of the college and with representative groups of students. In determining the legality of those codes, the designated administrators must review them carefully with the college's legal advisors.

At the same time it makes its periodic review of codes of student conduct, the institution should evaluate those procedures that are to be used to implement the codes, taking care that each employee of the college understands what constitutes disruptive behavior, to whom reports of disruptive behavior are to be transmitted sequentially, and the range of options and prerogatives available to those reporting incidents of disruption. If, because of the passage of time, the staff's recollection of these procedures becomes fuzzy, it probably behooves the designated administrator either to have them occasionally reviewed in departmental meetings or to develop and disseminate a procedural handbook that can be readily used to handle troublesome or disruptive incidents.

A DEFINITION OF DISRUPTION

In its broadest and most generic sense, the term disruption applies to behavior that persistently or grossly interferes with academic and administrative activities on campus. Ordinarily, such behavior actively hampers the ability of the other students to learn and of instructors to teach. Extreme forms of this behavior may even threaten the physical safety of students and staff.

The following is a specific, although not exhaustive, list of disruptive behaviors that commonly result in the administrative imposition of discipline:

1. Persistent or gross acts of willful disobedience or defiance toward college personnel.
2. Assault, battery, or any other form of physical abuse of a student or college employee.
3. Verbal abuse of a student or college employee.
4. Any conduct that threatens the health or safety of another individual (including any such action that takes place at an event sponsored or supervised by the college).
5. Theft or damage to the property of the college or another student.
6. Interference with the normal operations of the college (i.e., disruption of teaching and administrative functions, disciplinary procedures, pedestrian or vehicular traffic, or other college activities, including its public service functions).
7. Use of personal portable sound amplification equipment (e.g., radios and tape players) in a manner that disturbs the privacy of other individuals and/or the instructional program of the college.
8. Unauthorized entry into, or use of, college facilities.
9. Forgery, falsification, alteration or misuse of college documents, records, or identification.
10. Dishonesty such as cheating, plagiarism, or knowingly furnishing false information to the college and its officials.
11. Disorderly, lewd, indecent, or obscene conduct.
12. Extortion.
13. Breach of peace on college property or at any college sponsored or supervised function.
14. The use, possession, sale or distribution of narcotics or other dangerous illegal drugs on college property, or at any function sponsored or supervised by the college.
15. Possession or use of alcoholic beverages on college property, or at any function sponsored or supervised by the college. Obviously, many colleges may prefer to enforce this particular code on a flexible and selective rather than absolutist basis.
16. Illegal possession or use of firearms, explosives, dangerous chemicals, or other weapons on college property or at college sponsored activities.
17. Smoking in classrooms or other unauthorized campus areas.
18. Failure to satisfy college financial obligations.

19. Failure to comply with directions of college officials, faculty, staff, or campus security officers who are acting in performance of their duties.
20. Failure to identify oneself when on college property or at a college sponsored or supervised event, upon the request of a college official acting in the performance of his/her duties.
21. Gambling.
22. Sexual harassment or sexual and racial discrimination.
23. Violation of other applicable federal, state and local laws and college rules and regulations.
24. Theft or other abuse of computer time, including but not limited to:
    a. unauthorized entry into a file, to use, read, or change the contents, or for any other purpose.
    b. Unauthorized transfer of a file.
    c. Unauthorized use of another individual's identification and password.
    d. Use of computing facilities to interfere with the work of another student, faculty member or college official.
    e. Use of computing facilities to send obscene or abusive messages.
    f. Use of computing facilities to interfere with normal operation of the college computing system.
25. Abuse of the judicial system, including but not limited to:
    a. Failure to obey the summons of a judicial body or college official.
    b. Falsification, distortion, or misrepresentation of information before a judicial body.
    c. Disruption or interference with the orderly conduct of a judicial proceeding.
    d. Attempting to influence the impartiality of a member of a judicial body prior to, and/or during the course of, the judicial proceeding.
    e. Harassment (verbal or physical) and/or intimidation of a member of a judicial body prior to, during, and/or after a judicial proceeding.
    f. Failure to comply with the sanction(s) imposed under the student code.
    g. Influencing or attempting to influence another person to commit an abuse of the judicial system.
26. Hazing, defined as an act which endangers the mental or physical health or safety of a student, or which destroys or removes public or private property, for the purpose of initiation, admission into, affiliation with, or as a condition for continued membership in, a group or organization (Stoner and Cerminara, 1990).

Although many colleges are reluctant to oversee, regulate, or take responsibility for the behavior of students in off-campus settings, there have been instances when colleges have asserted their jurisdiction to punish students for extramural misconduct when the activity, in the college's estimation, has adversely affected the interests of the college community. In recent years the courts have accorded school officials rather wide latitude in determining whether an off-campus activity adversely affects the interests of the college community, recognizing that the college has a vital interest in the character of its students and therefore may regard a student's off-campus conduct as a reflection both of the student's character and fitness to be a member of the student body. Nevertheless, when off-campus misconduct takes place, it is usually advisable for college officials to determine the breadth of its jurisdiction on a case-by-case basis, considering the unique facts of each situation, "without the impossible problem of drafting language to cover every possible situation" (Stoner and Cerminara, 1990, p. 99).

FIVE PRINCIPLES

The disruptive student, whether emotionally disturbed or not, often angers, baffles, alarms, and immobilizes those college personnel who must cope directly and immediately with the disruptive behavior. In some cases the disruptive behavior has strikingly violated the code of student conduct and therefore clearly warrants disciplinary action on the part of the instructor or college administrator.

According to two legal authorities, there are five principles relating to discipline which emerge from case law (Close and Merchat, 1982).

1. The law does not expressly prohibit a college from disciplining a student for misconduct, even when that misconduct is directly related to his/her physical or mental disability.

For example, certain schizophrenic students might aver that since their hallucinatory and bizarre actions in class, although confessedly disruptive, are simply uncontrollable manifestations or symptoms of their mental illness, and therefore, in their view, immune from punishment. They are essentially mistaken, however, since, as indicated earlier, the college can legally impose disciplinary sanctions upon disruptive students even when the causality of their misconduct relates to a physical or mental disability.

2. Each college is required to provide "reasonable accommodation" to the physically/mentally disabled.

That is, major disruptions to the educational process may be met with disciplinary interventions, but minor disruptions need to be tolerated under the "reasonable accommodation" principle. In recent years, the principle of "reasonable accommodation" has been broadened by federal law and various education codes to require colleges to undertake to develop special programs, services, and facilities to meet the unique needs of students with physical or mental disabilities. As a result, many consternated administrators and instructors have raised questions about the extent to which traditional pedagogical methods and course content must be revamped in order to conform to the requirements of law.

As indicated, the principle of "reasonable accommodation" is most often applied to the requirement to develop special services, programs and facilities for students with mental or physical disabilities. Insofar as this principle is applied to the everyday functioning of the typical classroom, there is apparently little realistic cause for alarm. Obviously, students with auditory impairments should be provided with signers; students with visual impairments should be provided with braille materials; students with psychotic or panic disorders should be helped to attain psychological relief by being allowed inconspicuously and quickly to leave classes when necessary.

The principle of "reasonable accommodation" does not ordinarily mean, however, instituting major modifications in course content or teaching methods in order to enable students with disabilities to adjust to the rigors of the classroom environment. For example, mentally ill students who request that an instructor of abnormal psychology omit assigning a section of the textbook that deals with mental illness because reading such material is too emotionally upsetting, are probably requesting "unreasonable" accommodation from the instructor—who, after all, could not properly teach such a course without including relevant material on mental illness—and therefore their request most likely should be respectfully denied.

Obviously, colleges should attempt to make reasonable accommodations to the mentally and physically disabled student. In doing so, the following guidelines are recommended: When students request special accommodations on the basis of their disability, the college may, if it wishes, request that the students substantiate the disability by providing to the college psychiatric or medical records that attest to that disability. Then, if the college is satisfied that the request for special accommodations is both reasonable and practicable, it probably should be granted. If the disabled students, whose request for special accomodations have already been granted, are also disruptive students, and their disruptive behavior continues after they have received special accommodations, the college has a clear right to initiate disciplinary proceedings against the students.

If, for whatever reason, the college deems the disabled student's petition for special accommodations to be unacceptable at the outset, it must show good cause before denying such a request. If the request is ultimately denied *with good cause* and the disabled student subsequently behaves in a disruptive manner, the student is subject to the same disciplinary procedures and sanctions as are all other students.

3. **Each college is required to adopt rules and regulations regarding appropriate student behavior, spell out penalties for violation of these regulations, and clearly describe due process procedures for students who wish to appeal these penalties.**

The formal policy statement of the college should, therefore, provide a wide range of sanctions so that there is a series of alternatives to deal with the disruptive behavior of students. Alternatives for minor disruptions should include efforts to provide assistance to the students, for example, by referring them to a mental health professional on campus if available.

Two cases in particular have been referred to as "landmark" in affording students due process before disciplinary action is taken. In 1961, the case of *Dixon v. Alabama Board of Education,* required public institutions of higher education to extend the right of due process to students. In 1975, the case of *Goss v. Lopez,* in which a class action was brought by Ohio public high school students in the United States District Court for the Southern District of Ohio, affirmed the right of students to a hearing before public schools could impose such sanctions as suspension. On direct appeal, the United States Supreme Court reaffirmed this right (Stoner and Cerminara, 1990).

Because it regulates only governmental conduct, the due process clause is applicable only to public institutions. Many private institutions, however, have adopted similar provisions. The due process clause requires that students be given oral or written notice of the charges against them and, if they deny them, an explanation of the evidence the school authorities have and an opportunity to present their side of the story. The extent of the requisite notice depends upon the seriousness and complexity of the matter at hand. In minor matters, where a suspension will probably be imposed for no more than a day or two, the following rudimentary precautions must be taken against unfair or mistaken findings of misconduct and arbitrary exclusion from school:

a. there need be no delay between the time notice is given and the time of the hearing;

b. in the great majority of cases the disciplinarian may informally discuss the alleged misconduct with the student minutes after it has occurred;

c. in being given an opportunity to explain their version of the facts at this discussion, the students first must be told what they are accused of doing and what the basis of the accusation is;

d. since the hearing may occur almost immediately following the misconduct, notice and hearing should, as a a general rule, precede the removal of the student from the school; however,

e. there are recurring situations in which prior notice and hearing cannot be insisted upon;

f. students whose presence poses a continuing danger to persons or property or an ongoing threat of disrupting the academic process may be immediately removed from school; and in such cases,

g. the necessary notice and rudimentary hearing should follow as soon as practicable.

In more serious matters, which are likely to involve expulsion or suspension for more than a few days, the time between the notice and the hearing should be greater—at least five days—and the notice should extensively set forth the alleged facts that constitute the egregious conduct and the potential penalties involved.

4. **The sole basis for imposing disciplinary sanctions on a student is that student's behavior.**

A college may not discipline a student for being "mentally ill"— only for explicit *behavior* prohibited by the Student Code of Conduct. For this reason, it is extremely important that the student's exact behavior be documented in writing in accurate detail. All procedures and recommendations relating to the disciplinary process also need to be clearly documented.

5. **Mental health professionals must follow legally defined obligations to maintain confidentiality regarding client communications and records.**

In California however, *all* community college employees, including those who work as college psychotherapists, are required to report serious threats or risks of harm to self or others, as well as known instances of child abuse. (A section of the California education code sets forth such a requirement. My own survey of six other populous states—New York, Ohio, Michigan, Illinois, Massachusetts, and Pennsylvania—revealed that no such education code exists in those states, suggesting that this education code is perhaps peculiar to California). However, the duty of mental health professionals (including, of course, those who work in colleges), in particular, to warn in cases that involve serious threat or risk is based upon the legal principles established by the California Supreme Court in the case of *Tarasoff v. Board of Regents* (Steiner, 1989). These principles are now applicable in all other states as well, and have been mandated by the education codes in some jurisdictions.

DISCIPLINARY SANCTIONS

Establishment of codes and procedures that govern student conduct must be predicated upon a college administration's readiness to impose disciplinary sanctions for disruptive behavior. It is advantageous, therefore, that administrators who are responsible for carrying out disciplinary action endeavor to formulate and enforce a set of specified penalties for particular acts of disruption. Such a codified set of disciplinary sanctions need not be Hammurabian either in spirit or substance, but should be reasonably and gradationally commensurate with the seriousness of each act of disruption. In other words, the punishment should reasonably fit the "crime." For example, in developing such a hierarchy of disciplinary sanctions, a first-time case of plagiarism could perhaps result in a temporary suspension, whereas physical assault on an instructor or on-campus drug trafficking could conceivably result in expulsion.

In the interest of fairness and justice, a hierarchy that couples specific disruptive behaviors with proportionate sanctions should allow for extenuating circumstances that might mitigate disciplinary measures. Thus, a student who had just learned that a parent was diagnosed with a fatal illness and soon afterward "unprovokedly" defaced college property might, taking into account his grief-stricken state, receive a milder form of discipline than would otherwise be the case. Nevertheless, an administration that has in hand a ready-made set of reasonably proportionate and legally enforceable sanctions that specifically match a broad spectrum of potentially disruptive behaviors will reduce its own likelihood of administering discipline in a precipitate, muddled, or discriminatory manner.

Many incidents of disruptive behavior are quite ambiguous. It is often extremely difficult to unravel the truth about who, college employee or student, originally provoked or perpetuated a particular act of disruptiveness. As a result, the extent of a student's culpability, if any, may be extremely difficult to determine. Important questions may also arise regarding cultural differences that manifest themselves in atypical (for the college) styles and standards of dress, hygiene, speech, and behavior that can be too easily misconstrued as willful acts of misconduct. On the one hand, it is important to understand and respect cultural differences as much as possible to prevent ethnocentric biases from being used to punish those who are simply different. On the other hand, colleges must also be alert to the possibility that some students will use their cultural differences, whether contrived or real, as a pretext for conducting themselves in a genuinely abusive or disruptive manner.

In any case, when confronted with highly ambiguous disruptive situations that require consideration of extenuating circumstances, administrators often discover that a too-rigid adherence to the codes of student conduct may cause more harm than good. Often, an infusion of common sense and good judgment will provide a better resolution of the problem than the automatic invocation of a conduct code.

Chapter III

Recommended Procedures for Dealing With Incidents of Disruptions

The most common sources of reported incidents of disruption on nonresidential campuses are college faculty members who, by dint of their instructional duties, have the most extensive and, quite often, nerve-racking contact with disruption-prone students. Typically, by the time a faculty member reports an incident of disruption, the situation has reached quite serious, if not dire, proportions. There are several explanations for this.

First, faculty are often reluctant to report a disruptive student because they hope that benign inaction will lead to some form of spontaneous resolution. In other words, the instructor hopes that such students will somehow see the error of their ways and eventually shape up on their own. Second, instructors worry about the possibility that they will not be adequately supported by the college administration if they report a disruptive student. Worse, they sometimes exaggeratedly fear that the problem will be seen as a reflection of their own professional inadequacies and that a resultant investigation will only lead to the discovery of their own blameworthiness in the matter. Third, some instructors feel that most forms of discipline, no matter how mild and warranted, are excessively harmful to the disruptive student, who is seen as too fragile psychologically to withstand the pressure of any disciplinary measure. Finally, some instructors hesitate to complain about a disruptive student because they feel unprotected from reprisals from that student. Such fears, unfortunately, are not always unfounded.

By the time the disruptive student is finally reported to the administration, therefore, the behavior is usually recurrent, flagrant, and fairly insusceptible to change by any means other than a disciplinary measure. For this reason, if an administrator determines that a given student has been disruptive and deserves to be penalized, it is ordinarily important to consider the fairness and proportionality of the disciplinary sanction and also which form of discipline would best help the disruptive student take positive steps to correct his or her behavior.

ESSENTIAL PREROGATIVES

Faculty under pressure of coping with a disruptive student may forget that they, as instructors, have two essential prerogatives. The first, and most obvious, is to establish and implement academic standards. The second is to establish and enforce reasonable behavioral standards for each class. In carrying out this latter prerogative, the principle of reasonable accommodation should be followed—minor disruptions should be tolerated as well as possible, but major disruptions to the educational process should be met with disciplinary action. It is normally very reassuring to faculty to know that they do have rights and prerogatives and can insist upon conformity to reasonable codes of conduct within the jurisdiction of their own classes and offices.

A quite prevalent concern of faculty who report disruptive incidents, relates to the potential dangerousness of the disruptive student. Although this concern is sometimes disproportionate and groundless, it should never be dismissed out of hand. After all, many disruptive students are bigger, younger, and more vigorous than the instructor, and may, in extreme cases, have little compunction about using a weapon.

Even when there is no clear-cut evidence of a particular student's potential for violence or mayhem, no administrator or mental health practitioner can ever state with absolute certainty that the instructor is completely safe from harm. Instead, in disruptive situations that appear relatively innocuous, the instructor can be told that the student is probably not a potential threat to him or her. Should there be any doubt or apprehension on this score, however, he or she should take whatever precautions are necessary to avoid the possibility of being endangered. One example of such a precaution would be to arrange to meet with the disruptive student only in the company of other staff. Another would be to call upon the assistance of campus law enforcement officers to deal immediately with the student who demands to continue, unrelentingly, a rancorous discussion with the instructor.

When it appears there is a definite and imminent risk of physical harm to the instructor, the student should be reported at once to the designated administrator and to the campus police. If the campus does not have a law enforcement unit, the assistance of the city police or sheriff's office may be enlisted. In such cases, an administrative investigation and assessment should be undertaken immediately to determine the advisability of allowing the student to remain in the instructor's class. In California, based upon a relatively recent education code, instructors in community colleges may unilaterally (that is, without administrative approval) remove a disruptive student from two consecutive classes. This is often a handy intervention because it buys time until the matter can be more thoroughly and safely reviewed at the administrative level.

In cases that involve recurrent, blatant, and clearly unresolvable disruptive behavior but are not truly dangerous (except, possibly, to the morale and sanity of the instructor and the other students), a somewhat different tack may be necessary. Many of the students who fall into this category are demonstrably psychologically disabled and are simply unable to modify their disruptive behavior, even with the benefit of constant reminders, blandishments, or warnings.

In such cases, it may be best for an administrator to meet privately with these students, apprise them that they are at an unfortunate and insoluble impasse and that it may be in their interest to withdraw from the class (or college) as soon as possible. It may also be necessary to tell the student that at the present time the only disciplinary measure that is being taken is a warning, however, any further repetition of the disruptive behavior would probably result in a more severe form of penalty. To avoid the stigma of having that personally tarnishing outcome recorded in their academic records and to relieve themselves of the burden of having to struggle further with a clearly irremediable situation, such students might consider it advantageous to withdraw immediately.

In my own experience, when such students are approached in this way—especially when the administrator's manner is empathic but firm—they generally are fain to withdraw without severe penalty. A caveat: In such situations, administrators must be cautious not to cause students to waive their legal rights inappropriately; that is, they should avoid threatening or forcing students to do something they clearly object to doing.

The alternative and common practice of referring psychologically disabled students who have been disruptive to counselors or psychotherapists will be discussed later. Suffice to say here, however, that when mental health referrals are deemed appropriate, they should ordinarily be conducted on a voluntary and confidential basis and kept quite separate from disciplinary procedures.

DOCUMENTATION

In formally transmitting information about disruptive student behavior, instructors are advised to accompany their oral reports with written documentation of their observations. The documentation should be devoid of psychological jargon or speculation (e.g., "This person appears to be a paranoid schizophrenic" or "I think he's on drugs"). With as little editorializing as possible, the instructor should provide information that is specific and concrete, stressing only the student's unacceptable *behavior*. Finally, if instructors hold strong preferences regarding the ultimate disposition of their complaints, they should specify those preferences in their reports. This helps to remove some of the guesswork on the part of administrators who, in attempting to determine a proper course of action, will probably want to take the complainant's wishes into account. Upon completion, the documentation should be accurately dated and transmitted to the appropriate administrative officer for investigation and resolution.

When a disruptive incident has already spiraled dangerously out of control and an instructor needs immediate assistance to deal with it, that assistance should be readily available. The administration of a college has a twofold responsibility in this regard. First, it should ensure that emergency services (city or campus police or a mental health or crisis intervention team) are well in place and immediately enlistable. Second, all staff should be informed, in writing, about the procedures and resources that are to be used in the event of a dangerous emergency.

NON-INSTRUCTIONAL STAFF

Although this discussion has focused rather exclusively on the role of the instructor in handling disruptive students, instructional staff are obviously not the only college personnel who must deal with student disruptiveness. Counselors, support staff who work as custodians and secretaries, personnel who manage the bookstore, and administrative officers who are ultimately responsible for administering discipline are all, from time to time, involved in directly coping with disruptive student behavior. The principles outlined above for instructors should therefore also be valid and useful for noninstructional staff.

Support staff such as secretaries who work in the financial aid or registrar's office are often besieged and harassed by students who insist upon immediate attention to their personal needs. In some instances, students may resort to strident or intimidating tactics in order to gain an advantage. As a result, support staff who must directly deal with the unruly and minatory behavior of students frequently report that they feel frightened for their own safety. What precautions should they take?

First, they should meet with their supervisors and other campus officials who are responsible for their safety in order to develop a set of strategies and procedures for dealing with disruptive students. Then, a thorough evaluation of the physical work environment should be undertaken in order to ensure that the following safety features are in place: a means of ready egress so that staff may quickly and safely escape in the event of a dangerous emergency, a system of code words available to staff with which they may secretly alert others to disruptive crises, and, if necessary, a hidden and readily accessible buzzer that transmits a warning signal to a campus security office. Finally, support staff should have the same right that is accorded instructional staff to report students who have behaved disruptively toward them.

Support staff, like all other college personnel, are entitled to establish and enforce reasonable behavioral standards in their own work environment. Each college employee, irrespective of his or her particular professional assignment or work area, has the right to be treated with respect and dignity by students (and vice versa, of course). As one college official pointedly phrased the matter, "Suffering abuse is in no one's job description. No staff member or instructor should ... have to put up with bullying, intimidation, or violence" (Suzanne Belson, Concordia University, Montreal, personal communication).

THE AVERSION TO ADMINISTERING DISCIPLINE

Over the past several years I have consulted with many college officials who have reported, usually with considerable frustration, that their attempts to encourage their colleagues to report and carefully document cases of disruptive behavior have been thwarted by a widespread and somewhat inexplicable uncooperativeness. After exploring this dilemma with the resistive personnel themselves in workshops I have conducted, I discovered that the problem usually had little to do with a lack of knowledge, know-how, or technical ability regarding the college's official procedures for reporting disruptive conduct. Rather, there was considerable evidence to suggest that the resistances to reporting cases of student misconduct were related to subtle but powerful emotional factors that were instantaneously generated whenever staff were placed in the involuntary and unsavory position of disciplinarian. In the following discussion I will attempt to highlight and explain some of those factors.

First, discipline, especially admonitory discipline, tends to inflict psychic pain upon its recipients. Thus, unless the disciplinarian is an unregenerate sadist, he or she will administer discipline only with a degree of guilt, reluctance, and uneasiness. *Second*, many, if not most, college personnel easily lose sight of the potential positive value of discipline in coping with disruptive students. They often rather one-sidedly believe that discipline will necessarily serve only to exacerbate and escalate an already inflamed conflict, and may even hold to this position in the face of considerable, contrary, evidence that their prolonged inaction has inadvertently led to a serious escalation of disruption. *Third*, many academicians are drawn to academe by a desire to teach in a relatively disruption-free and untrammeled intellectual milieu and, therefore, react with dismay when they must deal with disciplinary situations.

It is important for those responsible for disciplining disruptive students to realize that discipline is not inherently cruel or immoral. Just and fair disciplinary measures, in providing a form of external control, may be exactly what a disruptive student needs to regain self-control. In some instances, decisive discipline may be the *only* antidote for dealing with an uncontrollably disruptive student. As one legal authority has pointed out, the imposition of a just punishment can affirm and enhance one's capacity to make moral choices (Pavela, 1985). Keeping this in mind, administrators who must mete out discipline to disruptive students might find it helpful to understand that the correct use of discipline quite often serves the interest of both the disruptive student and the college. When the discipline is successful, the student regains self-control and, it is hoped, remains in college; the college benefits by having one less disruptive student.

Nonetheless, it would be the height of self-serving Pollyannaism to assume that those disciplinary measures deemed good and beneficial by the college will necessarily be regarded favorably by the disruptive students themselves. It is, perhaps, more realistic to assume that many disruptive students will impenitently feel that the disciplinary sanctions imposed upon them are unwarranted, unfair, and unhelpful, even though they may change their behavior as a result. Nevertheless, because the college is seeking and requiring nothing more than a positive behavioral change, there is no particular reason for it to expect, demand, or attempt to engender in disruptive students a friendly attitude toward the discipline they have received.

At this juncture it might be helpful to point out, parenthetically, that college personnel who repeatedly and indiscriminately fail to report disruptive student conduct help, albeit unknowingly and inadvertently, to perpetuate disruptiveness. Through their passivity and inaction they become, to use an overemployed phrase, "co-dependents" of the disruptive student. Disruptive students who repeatedly observe that their misconduct is winked at and trivialized by college employees may logically assume the following: (1) Their disruptiveness is not really disruptive and bothers no one, (2) College employees are strangely indifferent to acts of disruption, and, therefore, (3) They have broad license to continue behaving disruptively. In such situations, as in the case of a spouse who passively contributes to the perpetuation of a destructive marriage by idly watching her husband drink and abuse his family for many years, the college employee who refuses to acknowledge and directly deal with disruptive student behavior unwittingly contributes to furthering that behavior.

THE SPECIAL BURDENS CARRIED BY ADMINISTRATORS

Administrators, in particular, have several additional burdens to deal with when confronted with reports of disruptive behavior. To carry out discipline properly, they must first carefully evaluate the report they have received. Ordinarily, they must ask themselves, "Is this report credible? Is the instructor who has reported the disruptive student perhaps exaggerating or manufacturing the gravity of the circumstances?" When there is doubt about the credibility or accuracy of the allegations, it may be necessary to hold a formal hearing—rather than, for example, meeting informally only with the student—in which witnesses can be questioned and allegedly disruptive students can fully defend themselves against the charges. (Guidelines for conducting formal hearings will be discussed in greater detail later, in the next chapter.) Based upon my own experience with the reports of such incidents, however, I would venture to say that in most cases of reported disruptiveness, the facts seem to speak for themselves. The complainant is normally a quite credible, reliable, and rational person, and, therefore, the designated administrator needs to act immediately and decisively to resolve the problem.

Some cases of reported disruptiveness, by their sheer complexity, will confound and discomfit even the most knowledgeable, astute, and self-assured administrator. There are college employees who, for whatever reasons, develop an unwavering animus for particular students and use their complaints against them to carry out personal vendettas. Sadistic and mendacious college personnel may deliberately lie and distort the facts when submitting complaints against students. Other college employees—racists, ageists, sexists, homophobes—may use their xenophobic prejudices to denounce and punish students who are different from themselves.

To complicate matters further, there are students who enter college with a seemingly personal agenda to make life miserable for everyone they happen to encounter. They are, regrettably, quite adroit in accomplishing their objective. At the first hint of an administrative investigation of their misconduct, they become litigious, threatening to file an expensive law suit against the college for the supposed injustices about to be inflicted upon them.

In short, the enormously complex personal idiosyncrasies of staff and students alike, when considered during an administrative investigation of a complicated case of alleged disruptiveness, might lead one to conclude that the administrator best suited to this Olympian task is an individual who is doubly endowed with the patience of a Job and the wisdom of a Solomon.

Administrators often feel stymied and thwarted because some instructors who report disruptive students have not followed due process. In other words, those instructors who are petitioning for administrative intervention with disruptive students have not given sufficient warning to the offending students about their behavior or have not adequately documented their observations since the inception of the objectionable behavior. Administrators rightly consider themselves hamstrung when there has been little adherence to due process. If they proceed with disciplinary procedures under these circumstances, they may be professionally and personally vulnerable during a judicial investigation or hearing.

Two courses of action are available to help obviate this dilemma somewhat. First, if administrators discover that their staffs are too regularly overlooking the need to follow due process, it behooves them to develop written materials and in-service training activities so that all employees can become familiar with the need and procedures for fulfilling these requirements. Second, when immediate intervention is necessary and due process has not heretofore been followed, administrators, if necessary, can accelerate, condense, and streamline the entire investigative/administrative process. They may first request that instructors quickly and retroactively document the course of disruptive events and promptly transmit their written reports to the administration, then suggest that the instructor refer the student to the appropriate administrator for an immediate interview and official review of the matter. If necessary, administrators may consider imposing an immediate "interim suspension" upon the student who poses an acute and imminent danger to the campus community in order to defuse the element of risk quickly and to allow more time to resolve the disruptive crisis.

A further complication that fosters an aversion for and delay in administering discipline is that most college administrators who serve as disciplinarians are middle-management executives—often the deans of students. They do not possess the ultimate authority for resolving certain cases of disruptive behavior in a way that is commensurate with their official responsibilities for meting out discipline. When faced with complicated disciplinary cases, administrators will often turn to their administrative superiors for help. The latter may, in turn, consult the college attorney for a more authoritative legal opinion. Implementing these multiple consultations will sometimes cause protracted and frustrating delays in resolving the disruptive crisis.

To complicate matters further, the final opinions and recommendations of the legal staff or of the highest ranking administrative officers of the college may be inimical to the interests or desires of the college employee who originally reported the disruptive student. For example, instructors who have been confronted with highly disruptive and possibly dangerous students and are virtually at the end of their emotional tether will probably want such students removed and barred from their classes at once. The college attorney or a high-ranking administrator, however, may recommend that the college delay action until the instructors more adequately fulfill the requirements of documentation and due process.

Administrators who are at the center of this crossfire of conflicting demands and perspectives are on the horns of a rather nasty dilemma. If, in deference to a legal opinion, they refuse to fulfill the terms of the instructor's petition for help, they can be subject to accusations of moral spinelessness and dereliction of duty. If, however, they opt to grant the instructor's request immediately by intervening despite an inadequate adherence to due process, they may later find themselves rather far out on a tenuous legal limb, with few institutional allies or safeguards to protect them from students who might seek legal retribution.

In my role as a consultant to various colleges regarding disruptive student behavior I have often observed considerable delays in the resolution of many of those cases that required consultation with the colleges' attorneys. Some of these delays were entirely understandable since attorneys ordinarily have very busy and crowded schedules and a case of an individual disruptive student may not be among their highest priorities. Moreover, complicated cases of student misconduct may require many hours of legal research and investigation before a final determination can be made. However, since such delays are quite common, it is imperative, I believe, that faculty (who often are on tenterhooks while nervously awaiting an administrative decision), be regularly apprised of the status of their complaint.

More problematic, however, are the stresses and disjunctions that take place when the attorney confers a legal opinion that is clearly inimical to the interests of the complainant, such as when an instructor each day must have frightening encounters with a disruptive student and the college attorney recommends a glacially slow, non-disciplinary form of resolution to the problem. Such disjunctions between college employees who file complaints about disruptive students and college attorneys who ordinarily have a highly influential advisory role in the adjudication of such cases are not uncommon. What accounts for these disjunctions?

First, of course, it is possible that the complainants, in filing a complaint, may not have sufficiently understood or respected a student's academic or constitutional rights and therefore it is left up to the college attorney to protect those rights by disallowing the complaint.

However, upon further investigation, we usually find that there are far more subtle and complicated reasons for the many cases of troublesome disjunction between college complainants and college attorneys. One legal authority (Smith, 1988) offers the following caveat: Just because someone is a college attorney does not mean that he or she possesses the requisite skills in such matters. College and university law is a specialty, and although recent graduates of law schools may be helpful, ideally a college attorney should have at least five years of experience in the practice of law and be well versed in the legal field of personnel, negligence, and, if it is a public institution, governmental operations. A persuasive personality and strong trial experience can also be boons to the college attorney who will be regularly engaging in the difficult processes of negotiation.

According to these standards, many attorneys who represent colleges clearly do not yet have the legal experience or expertise to fulfill the arduous requirements of their assignment. To what extent this generally hampers the proper and expeditious resolution of cases involving disruptive students is unclear but certainly requires further study on a case-by-case basis.

Another writer on this subject (Stoner, 1992, personal communication) has suggested that the disjunction and miscommunication that frequently arise between college attorneys and college employees are due to the differences in their educational and experiential backgrounds. Because many college attorneys spend little time on the campus itself, because they are "outside counsel" or have other conflicting duties, and because they do not become regularly or intimately involved in matters that pertain to student affairs, they may lack the essential intuition and insights about the inner workings of the campus community that one naturally acquires by simply working "in the system." Thus, as an "outsider" to student affairs legal issues and processes, a college attorney may be at a disadvantage when called upon to give legal advice concerning complicated cases of student disruptiveness, especially if he or she is the sole attorney for the college and may therefore have too little time or available manpower properly to investigate such cases.

In my own experience in dealing with these cases I have observed another institutional dynamic that seems important, if not decisive, in determining their final legal disposition. From carefully listening to the conversations and watching the actions of some college attorneys who have been consulted about cases of disruptive students, I have discerned that they have been preoccupied, above all else, with the specter of lawsuits arising out of their own actions. Although my own eye may be jaundiced and overly cynical, I have often had the impression that the attorney's final opinion on these cases was formulated largely on the basis of a cold calculation regarding the potential litigiousness of the defendant/student. And, where students were indeed regarded as highly litigious, the legal recommendation disproportionately favored some form of leniency toward them—a kind of game of jurisprudential roulette, with the attorney, more often than not, betting on the student, rather than the complainant, as the more likely principal to sue the college.

If I am correct in my observation, and this practice continues, I foresee a time when college employees will "catch on" to this handy formula for legally resolving cases of student disruptiveness and, unfortunately, will begin to hire their own attorneys to litigate cases against their own colleges on the grounds that their rights and safety have not been sufficiently protected from disruptive students by the college. If such a scenario comes to pass, there is certainly reason to believe that it will have a profound effect upon how cases of student misconduct will be adjudicated by college attorneys in the future.

AN INSTITUTIONAL ANOMALY

One method of escape that has been commonly used by administrators who feel trapped between the importunate demands of faculty for immediate disciplinary intervention and the demands of a more dilatory system of due process is to refer disruptive students to counselors and mental health practitioners for evaluation and/or therapy in hopes that this will somehow ameliorate or resolve the crisis. Although many administrative referrals of students to counselors and psychotherapists are quite appropriate, especially when the students themselves indicate a desire to receive psychological services, referrals of students who have been disruptive (and are being referred *because* they have been disruptive) are usually inadvisable and of little value. Depending on the degree of force and coercion employed in carrying out such a referral, this particular strategy may also be of questionable legality as well.

It is common for administrators to refer disruptive students to counselors and therapists, not simply to escape a legal dilemma, but because they think it is somehow kinder, and perhaps less damaging, to students to have their difficulties viewed as mental health, rather than disciplinary, problems.

This particular strategy usually results in an institutional anomaly: Therapists and counselors (whose job it is to guide and heal) are asked or required, under administrative pressure, to assume quasi-disciplinary functions and responsibilities; and administrators (whose job, among others, it is to administer discipline) are, instead, counseling disruptive students about their need for mental health services. This anomaly is especially apparent when the evident purpose and expectation of the administrative referral are to have the therapist or counselor, by hook or crook, "stop" the student from being disruptive. Although there may be nothing wrong with an administrator's recommending psychotherapy to a student, it is ordinarily inappropriate and counterproductive to use such recommendations as a handy substitute for appropriate disciplinary action. I will return to this subject in a later chapter, which describes the role of a college mental health program in dealing with disruptive students.

To appreciate better the implications of such institutional anomalies, I believe it helpful to consider a few trenchant caveats proferred by Halleck (1971):

1. When society decides that a person is behaving unreasonably enough to be a psychiatric patient, it simply makes a judgment, which must be sanctioned by professionals, about the maladaptive basis of that person's conduct and assumes that the person who behaves in such a manner is troubled or unhappy. In some instances, the individual may not feel troubled; therefore, he may be placed in the patient role involuntarily (R.L. Arstein, MD, in a 1991 personal communication notes that it is also true that in most states "society" supports the idea that mental health professionals sometimes may need to "place someone in the patient role involuntarily," at least briefly).

2. The judgment of unreasonable suffering or behavior is always a value judgment, frequently based on arbitrary and shifting criteria.
3. The psychiatric profession has often loaned its talents to perpetuate unsubstantiated belief systems or myths. Inadvertently, therapists and counselors sometimes use their positions to deter society from confronting and dealing with inequities in the distribution of power.

A FEW ALTERNATIVES

Waiting for Sufficient Grounds

Instructors whose requests for immediate administrative intervention with a disruptive student are denied are normally faced with several unpalatable choices. They may accept the administrative decision and painfully bide their time with a disruptive student until the disruptiveness either subsides or further escalates. In the event that it persists or escalates, the ensuing escalation may provide the college with sufficient grounds for administrative action. Instructors will then be able to petition the college again, but now with stronger evidence of the student's continuing disruptiveness and, the instructor hopes, provide a more convincing record of their adherence to due process.

Filing Criminal Charges

A second choice. If instructors consider themselves extremely endangered by the retention of a disruptive student in their class and still cannot secure administrative support for removing that student, and *when the student's behavior seems to be in violation of the law (e.g., a misdemeanor or felony)*, instructors may certainly exercise their civil and constitutional rights by filing criminal charges against the student with the local police department or sheriff's office. For example, in California, a section of the state penal code makes it a crime willfully to threaten to commit a crime that will result in death or great bodily injury to another person. Another section of the penal code makes it a punishable public offense directly to threaten officers and employees of public or private educational institutions (West's California Codes, 1990).

Considering the unequivocal dangerousness of some acts of student misconduct, it is imperative that college employees who are dealing with students whose disruptive behavior may be in violation of the law periodically review the penal codes of their own states and municipalities to determine the proper grounds for reporting potential crimes and to enlist the intervention of the judicial system in resolving on-campus acts of criminality.

Finally, in lieu of, or in addition to, filing criminal charges against students who appear to violate the law, college employees can—especially in cases that require the immediate imposition of security measures—seek the assistance of the courts in having a restraining order placed upon the endangering student.

Taking Legal Action Against One's Own College

A far more extreme and controversial step for college employees who believe they are unduly imperiled by the inaction of their own colleges in dealing with a particularly disruptive student is to threaten or actually carry out, in their own behalf, a legal action against the college. Such an action would probably be based upon the charge that the student is being permitted by the college to interfere seriously with the civil or constitutional rights of the employee. Obviously, such an extreme measure can be fraught with considerable personal and professional risks and, therefore, should ordinarily not be undertaken without a good deal of circumspection and the benefit of expert legal advice.

Considering the many reasons that underlie a general aversion to discipline, it is understandable, as Pavela (1985) has stressed, that the administration of punishment often requires considerable moral courage.

Chapter IV

Due Process for the Disruptive Student

One of the clearest and most authoritative discussions of due process has appeared in an article co-authored by Stoner and Cerminara (1990). While fine points of rights and procedure may vary from institution to institution, their work describes typical campus disciplinary processes today. For the benefit of readers who have not read this excellent article I will summarize their legal findings and recommendations.

1. Any member of the college community may file charges

Any member of the college community may file charges against any student for misconduct. Charges should be prepared in writing and transmitted to the college official (the judicial advisor) responsible for the administration of the college's judicial system. It is my observation that the practice varies regarding the length of limitation periods—a college "statute of limitations" that determines how soon after an incident the complainant must file charges—ranging from two days at one college to one year at another.

2. The judicial advisor may conduct an investigation

The judicial advisor may conduct an investigation to determine if the charges have merit and/or if they can be disposed of administratively by mutual consent of the parties involved on a basis acceptable to the judicial advisor. Such disposition shall be final and there shall be no subsequent proceedings. If the charges cannot be disposed of by mutual consent, the judicial advisor may later serve in the same matter as a member of the judicial body.

Where possible, it is preferable that the participants in the disciplinary process have had no prior contact with the student(s) involved, but the courts have recognized that on many, especially smaller, campuses, it is not possible completely to sanitize the process in this manner.

3. All charges shall be presented to the accused student

All charges shall be presented to the accused student in written form. A time shall be set for a hearing, not less than five nor more than fifteen calendar days after the student has been notified. Maximum time limits for scheduling of hearings may be extended at the discretion of the judicial advisor. This flexibility permits the college to accommodate disruptions in the college schedule such as holiday and vacation breaks, and examination periods. In fairness to accused students, they should by all means be allowed to adequately prepare their defenses.

4. Hearings should be conducted by a judicial body

Hearings should be conducted by a judicial body according to the following guidelines:

a. Hearings should normally be conducted in private. At the request of the student, and subject to the discretion of the judicial advisor, a member of the student press may attend the hearing but does not have the privilege of participating.

b. Admission of any person to the hearing shall be at the discretion of the judicial body and/or its judicial advisor.

c. In hearings involving more than one accused student, the judicial advisor may permit the hearings concerning each student to be conducted separately.

d. The complainant and the accused have the right to be assisted by any advisor they choose, at their own expense. The advisor may be an attorney. However, complainants and/or the accused are responsible for presenting their own cases and, therefore, advisors are not permitted to speak or to participate directly in any hearing before a judicial body. In other words, if the advisor is an attorney, he or she is not allowed to cross-examine witnesses.

e. The complainant, the accused and the judicial body shall have the privilege of presenting witnesses, subject to the right of cross-examination by the judicial body.

f. Pertinent records, exhibits and written statements may be accepted as evidence for consideration by a judicial body at the discretion of the chairperson. I have been asked by instructors if it might be appropriate to videotape a class in which one of their students has been behaving disruptively in order to obtain visual "proof" of the student's misconduct. Without hesitation, I have replied with an emphatic "No!"

My reasoning is as follows: If the videotaping is done without their knowledge and consent, all students in the class would have good reason to believe that the surreptitious filming constituted an invasion of their privacy. On the other hand, even if, for some bizarre reason, all the students, including the student under suspicion, actually consented to have their class filmed for the purpose of acquiring evidence against someone, it is very unlikely that anyone in that class would behave authentically under the circumstances.

In any case, considering the outcome of the first Rodney King trial, it seems that many persons do not believe in the verisimilitude of cinematographic evidence. Although filming a disruptive student may be legally permissible under certain special circumstances, its usual impracticalities, in my opinion, far outweigh its usefulness as a means of gathering evidence. Therefore, should an instructor be disposed to filming a class in order to acquire incriminating evidence against a disruptive student, I think it highly advisable that he or she first seek legal and/or administrative advice before proceeding.

g. All procedural questions are subject to the final decision of the chairperson of the judicial body.

h. After the hearing, the judicial body shall determine (by majority vote if the judicial body consists of more than one person) whether the student has violated each section of the student code which the student is charged with violating.

i. The judicial body's determination shall be made on the basis of whether it is more likely than not that the accused student violated the student code.

Several legal principles also serve as hearing guidelines: *First*, the hearing need not be open to the public. *Second*, neither the Federal Rules of Evidence nor any state's rules of evidence apply in student disciplinary proceedings. *Third*, although there are some allowable exceptions, a student need not be permitted to be represented by counsel at most student disciplinary hearings. However, even in exceptional cases that require that the accused be permitted representation by an attorney, counsel may be restricted to an advisory role.

5. *There shall be a single verbatim record*

There shall be a single verbatim record, such as a tape recording, of all hearings before a judicial body. The record shall be the property of the college.

6. *Violations of the student code*

Except in the case of a student charged with failing to obey the summons of a judicial body or college official, no student may be found to have violated the student code solely because the student failed to appear before a judicial body.

SANCTIONS

1. *Sanctions against students*

The following sanctions may, typically, be imposed upon any student found to have violated the student codes. At most institutions, the gradations of applicable sanctions increase with the severity of the offense.

a. *Warning*—A notice in writing to the student that the student is violating or has violated institutional regulations.

b. *Probation*—A written reprimand for violation of specified regulations. Probation is for a designated period of time and includes the probability of more severe disciplinary sanctions if the student is found to be violating any institutional regulation(s) during the probationary period.

c. *Loss of privileges*—Denial of specified privileges for a designated period of time.

d. *Fines*—Previously established and published fines may be imposed.

e. *Restitution*—Compensation for loss, damage or injury. This may take the form of appropriate service and/or monetary or material replacement.

f. *Discretionary Sanctions*—Work assignments, service to the college or other related discretionary assignments (such assignments must have the prior approval of the judicial advisor). In my view, however, the college should take strict precautions to insure that work which is undertaken in order to meliorate punishment is entirely voluntary or the college could rightly be charged with imposing unconstitutional, involuntary servitude upon students.

g. *Residence Hall Suspension*—Separation of the student from the residence halls for a definite period of time, after which the student is eligible to return. Conditions for readmission may be specified.

h. *Residence Hall Expulsion*—Permanent separation of the student from the residence halls.

i. *College Suspension*—Separation of the student from the college for a definite period of time, after which the student is eligible to return. Conditions for readmission may be specified.

j. *College Expulsion*—Permanent separation of the student from the college. (At many colleges the sanction of expulsion cannot be imposed without a formal ratification by the college's board of governors or its equivalent governing body.

2. *Multiple sanctions*

More than one of the sanctions listed above may be imposed for any single violation.

3. *Sanctions as part of records*

Other than college expulsion, disciplinary sanctions shall not be made part of the student's permanent academic record, but shall become part of the student's confidential record. Upon graduation, the student's confidential record may be expunged of disciplinary actions other than residence-hall expulsion.

4. Sanctions against groups
The following sanctions may be imposed upon groups or organizations:

a. *Those sanctions listed above* in 1, *a* through *e*.

b. *Deactivation*—Loss of all privileges, including college recognition, for a specified period of time.

Finally, to determine whether the allegedly disruptive student or organization has violated the college's standards and warrants some form of sanctioning, a standard of proof must be established. The standard of proof required in student disciplinary cases usually is defined as the greater weight of credible evidence, in contrast to the standard of proof required in criminal matters, which is defined as beyond a reasonable doubt (Ragle and Justice, 1989).

We now leave Stoner and Cerminara's model student disciplinary code in order to take up the matter of disclosure and student privacy.

DISCLOSURE

Following a student's hearing for allegedly violating a code(s) of student conduct, it is likely that the complainants will eagerly wish to be apprised of the outcome. Obviously, their motivation for coveting this information is not simply morbid curiosity. They have played an instrumental role in reporting the accused student and therefore have a pressing and legitimate need to be told something about the final disposition of their complaints.

After all, if the student, for example, has been accused of violating a code of conduct because he has repeatedly behaved disruptively in class and the judicial body has ruled to suspend that student immediately, the instructor must be informed of that decision in order to exercise his or her legitimate right to bar the student from the classroom. If the instructors are not privy to that essential knowledge, students conceivably could return to the classroom and rather easily hornswoggle them into believing that they were somehow exonerated of all charges and had full judicial approval to remain in their class.

What, then, are the ground rules for informing complainants of the final decisions of the judicial body? Some state education codes protect student privacy. A more pervasive piece of legislation governing matters of student privacy is the Family Education Rights and Privacy Act (FERPA), often referred to as the Buckley Amendment.

Under FERPA, the college is permitted to release "directory information" about a student, such as a student's name, address, telephone number, date and place of birth, major field of study, participation in officially recognized activities and sports, weight and height of members of athletic teams, dates of attendance, degrees and awards received, and the most recent educational agency or institution attended by the student. It is required, however, that every institution give "public notice" of the categories of such information it designates as "directory information," and must allow a reasonable period of time after such notice for the student to notify the institution that "he or she does not want any or all of those types of information about the student designated as directory information" (34 CFR 99.37).

Under FERPA, other sorts of information from educational records cannot be released. There are two exceptions. The first is a limited exception made for law enforcement cases. The other exception is made in cases that present a physical danger to other persons. Since it would appear that these two exceptions would not be especially applicable in most cases of disruptive students for whom disciplinary hearings are conducted, on what other basis could complainants receive information from a judicial officer regarding the results of a disciplinary hearing that would not cause the college to run afoul of the Buckley Amendment?

Evidently, there is another legal principle that may be used in order to allow judicial officers to disclose the findings of disciplinary hearings to complainants and/or other institutional personnel. If, in the estimation of the judicial advisor, college staff require such information in order to carry out their professional assignments safely and satisfactorily, they may be apprised of the disciplinary rulings of the judicial body (M. Smith, personal communication).

In addition, a recent amendment to FERPA (20 U.S.C. Sec. 1232g; 18 U.S.C. Sec. 16) provides that the institution may disclose to the victim of a crime of violence (who is usually a student) the results of any disciplinary proceeding conducted by the institution against the alleged perpetrator of the crime. For this purpose, the law defines a "crime of violence" as one involving the use, or threatened use, of force against the person or property of another person, or any felony that carries with it a substantial risk that physical force may be used against a person or property in the course of committing the offense.

For those judicial officers who may view their own discretionary latitude in such cases with some trepidation, it might offer some comfort to know: (1) The sole penalty for failing to abide by the terms of the Buckley Amendment is that an educational institution might lose its eligibility for federal funding, (2) Apparently, no institution has ever lost federal funds as a result of violating FERPA and, (3) FERPA does not give anyone a private right to bring a damage suit against an institution or person for failing to abide by the terms of the Buckley Amendment.

The reader who wishes to acquire a more precise understanding of the legal scope of FERPA is advised to consult Michael Clay Smith's book, *Coping with Crime on Campus*, especially pages 74-78.

One final caveat may be in order: A loose-tongued gossipmonger who casually broadcasts the findings of confidential hearings to the campus or off-campus community may subject himself or herself to civil liability.

Chapter V

Disruptiveness in Residence Halls

It is generally recognized that the quality and extent of disruptiveness in college residence halls reflect, approximate, and usually follow the patterns of violence and social disarray in the extramural world. Since college students are products of a highly violent society in which they have spent their entire lives there is no logical reason to consider them entirely immune from various forms of violence, as either victims or perpetrators.

As Palmer (1993) has pointed out, community housing patterns in the United States are strongly related to race, ethnicity, and socioeconomic status. Thus, the college or university residence hall, which blends together persons of many races, religions, lifestyles, and value systems, may represent the most culturally diverse environment in which many of today's college students will *ever* live.

When large numbers of persons reside together in concentrated proximity, it is inevitable that interpersonal tensions, misunderstandings, incivilities, and disharmonies will arise, at times reaching serious proportions. The college residence hall, which brings together, in daily contact, many persons of diverse social backgrounds and sensibilities, can of course provide positive socializing experiences for many students. However, the bustle of regular and sometimes unwilling interaction with large numbers of persons with a wide range of personality styles and cultural values can instill in some students intense fears and resentments that may cause them to behave disruptively or even violently.

There are many students who are particularly susceptible to the pressures of the new and (for them) somewhat alien social environment of the residence hall. Callow and lacking in social skills, these students may approach others with an excessive awkwardness or high level of self-centeredness that may be perceived as off-putting and offensive. Many students, particularly those who, prior to college, have been used to having their personal property and space entirely under their own control and dominion, may find it extremely difficult to share and negotiate with others over territorial matters. When disputes arise, these students may find it especially difficult to tolerate or even acknowledge the rights and needs of others, responding with both a lack of resiliency and an increased determination to dictate the terms of settling any and all territorial disagreements.

At many colleges, racist attitudes and behavior of certain students have been a source of deep concern and unrest. For example, at one university an African-American woman from a lower socio-economic background shared a dormitory suite with three white women from relatively affluent backgrounds. When one of the white students had her wallet stolen she automatically suspected and accused the black student of theft. Although she did not press charges against the black student (who, as it turned out, was demonstrably innocent of the allegations) her subsequent behavior was marked by blatant acts of bigotry.

She repeatedly told the black student not to take her remarks personally, but it probably would be better if she found other living quarters. As well, the black student was told by her white roommates that she could no longer share their personal belongings and was generally treated by them with suspicion and contempt. Yet, when they were informed by residential staff that their conduct could easily be construed as racist, they insisted that their behavior toward the black student was uninfluenced by racial prejudice.

Practically any crime or act of violence that is perpetrated in the "outside world" can and does take place within the confines of college campuses. Cases of rape, particularly date rape, have reached almost epidemic proportions on college campuses throughout the country. A 1985 national survey by Koss, Gidycz, and Wisniewski (1987) of 7,000 students on 35 campuses revealed the following findings:

1. One in eight women have been raped; and
2. Eighty-five percent of these incidents occurred among students who knew one another and 5% of the attacks involved more than one assailant; and
3. Three-quarters of the victims of acquaintance rape did not identify their experience as rape and none of the males involved believed they had committed a crime; and
4. Forty-five percent of the males who committed acquaintance rape said they would repeat the experience; and
5. More than one-third of the women raped did not discuss the experience with anyone and more than 90 percent of them did not report the incident to the police.

As residence staff have, over the years, generally developed more awareness of what constitutes rape, there has been a nationwide increase in the reporting of incidents of sexual violence, harassment and victimization.

An ongoing and sometimes acute concern of colleges that maintain residence halls has been the verbal, emotional and even physical abuse of residence staff. Some students engage in teasing and harassing behavior toward resident assistants (RAs). They may attempt, in some instances, to obstruct and undermine their work assignments. Some of this behavior may be retaliatory, reprisals for incurring some form of discipline as a result of past inappropriate behaviors. Minority RAs may become victims of racial slurs; female RAs may encounter sexual obscenities as well as other forms of sexually predatory behavior.

Malicious and sometimes dangerous pranks are quite common in residence halls. At one college, students considered it a hilarious and harmless prank to throw heavy furniture from the upper story windows of a dormitory, entirely disregarding the possibility that this wacky form of jollification might seriously injure or even kill someone.

It is not uncommon for RAs to encounter students who are extremely homophobic. Some of these students may treat their gay and lesbian peers with scorn and contempt, openly ridiculing or ostracizing them in the residential halls. As one might expect with homophobic students, the language they use when referring to gay and lesbian students is often highly derogatory and degrading.

As most RAs readily acknowledge, alcohol and drug use are extremely prevalent (albeit covertly, in many instances) in college residential facilities. The excessive use of drugs and alcohol is a well known contributor to acts of vandalism, rowdiness and, in some extreme situations, physical assaults and violence upon both staff and students.

Obviously, not all forms of disruptive or troublesome behavior are directed toward others or toward the physical environment. It is quite common for RAs to encounter students with dangerous eating disorders such as anorexia and bulimia. The anorectic student may engage in self-starvation to such a dangerous extent that the college RA may need to request administrative and/or medical intervention. Bulimic students may also arouse deep and widespread concern in the residential hall, among both staff and students, because of their bingeing-purging habits.

The suicidal student who lives in the residential hall is often a source of intense and continual concern. Such students frighten and often induce considerable guilt in their residential peers who feel helpless yet responsible for dealing with suicidal students' tenuous regard for their own lives.

Certain forms of seemingly innocuous behavior can actually be highly detrimental to some students who live in residential facilities. Many RAs have observed that large numbers of students spend many hours each day watching television, especially soap operas. At times, this excessive TV-watching appears to be a form of addiction with certain deleterious effects.

First, it may overly induce wool-gathering tendencies that make it difficult for some students to return actively and realistically to the task of dealing with the vicissitudes of real life. *Second*, the pastime of sitting before a television watching soap operas hour after hour is time that is not used for either creatively interacting with others or for studying. Thus, the opiatic effect of protracted television-viewing may dull the senses, reduce opportunities for positive and enriching social relationships, and rob the student of time that might be more productively spent keeping abreast of scholastic tasks.

DEALING WITH HARASSMENT OF RESIDENTIAL STAFF

As Rickarn (1989) has pointed out, RAs who become victims of abuse or harassment may blame themselves for being victimized. They may unwarrantedly believe they have somehow provoked the student into treating them harassingly, and as a result, experience feelings of personal failure and despair. Complicating their situation are feelings of divided loyalty, to both their student charges and to the college authorities for whom they work. Thus, they may be reluctant to report disruptive or harassing incidents for fear that they will be considered duplicitous by the disruptive student.

At times, they may also fail to report disruptive students because of a fear of legal or physical reprisals. Some RAs tend to rationalize their unwillingness to report abusive behavior by somehow considering harassment to be their just due, an unpalatable aspect of their job that just "comes with the territory." All in all, when RAs regularly absorb and resign themselves to excessive abuse from students, serious morale problems result that can contribute to an escalation of staff victimization.

Countermeasures to Harassment

There is much that can be done to sensitize and empower staff to deal with student harassment. For example:

1. Provide training and supervision to residential staff that enables them to recognize and define abusive behavior.

2. Provide ongoing supervision and consultation to staff that supports and nurtures their ability to act affirmatively when confronted with student harassment.

3. Develop programs and training experiences that assist staff in understanding the nature and underlying causes of disruptive behavior.

4. Assist RAs in understanding how and when to make referrals of emotionally troubled students to professional psychotherapeutic services. As Boswinkel (1986) has suggested, making such referrals can

be the most challenging part of assisting students with serious psychological problems.
5. Providing consistent and reliable safeguards to staff that will sufficiently protect them from legal and physical reprisals. Ordinarily, such protection can be optimized by providing residential staff with the ready assistance of various campus offices: public safety, judicial affairs, counseling, and, of course, the director of housing.
6. Assist staff in identifying those areas of the physical environment that seem to breed dangerous and disruptive incidents (such as unlocked dormitory doors and overly darkened areas) and help them to eliminate or at least diminish the dangerousness of these areas.
7. Assist staff by investigating, expediting and resolving reported incidents of disruption in a prompt, thorough and judicious manner. Unfortunately, the Buckley Amendment (FERPA) probably precludes the disclosure of the outcome of the disciplinary action to other students even when they are employed as staff members by the university (unless, of course, other students are placed at serious personal risk by non-disclosure). However, a recent decision by the Supreme Court of Georgia held that the results of disciplinary hearings are discoverable under state open meetings and open records acts (*Red & Black Pub. Co. v. Bd. of Regents*, 427 S.E. 2d 257 [1993]), and if the information is reported by the press, anyone can discuss it.
8. Impress upon residential staff that suffering abuse is not in their job description and that reporting abusive students is not an act of betrayal or duplicity.
9. Encourage RAs to develop in the residence halls a positive community with clear policies and procedures that help to promote an atmosphere in which the civil and personal rights of students are upheld and respected.
10. Familiarize the RAs with the general policies and procedures of the college, including the code of student conduct, in order that they fully understand their rights and prerogatives in dealing with disruptive students.

DEALING WITH THE PROBLEM OF RAPE

There are a large number of strategies and methods for dealing with the problem of rape, both preventative and reactive, that can be effectively employed within the setting of a college residential hall. For example:
1. Residential staff need to be informed that acquaintance rapes and sexual assaults happen in dormitories and that they will therefore be expected to be alert to this possibility and to report any and all incidents of this nature to the appropriate institutional authorities.
2. RAs should be trained and supported to teach rape prevention practices to potential victims and to develop programs that inform po-

tential assailants of the civil and criminal liabilities that could result from the perpetration of rape or sexual assault.
3. As Parrot (1991) has suggested, one way to decrease the incidence of rape is to publicize data regarding acquaintance rapes that have occurred on the college campus. Therefore, residential staff need to be informed about how to compose, edit, organize and disseminate literature on the on-campus incidence of acquaintance rapes that will be relevant and useful to students.
4. RAs need to be helped to coordinate their rape-prevention efforts with the other offices of the college campus as well as with the off-campus community. For example, they can be encouraged to have guest speakers from the campus and off-campus communities— nurses, doctors, psychotherapists, students, police, etc.—to discuss with residents rape prevention and rape treatment.
5. Since the excessive consumption of alcohol is a common contributor to rape, residential staff should be encouraged to organize activities (e.g., parties) at which alcohol is not served yet entertaining fun is available. Ideally, these activities would eventually serve to replace those parties at which heavy drinking usually takes place.
6. The college administrative staff should immediately investigate reports of rape, and in cases where the allegations are demonstrably valid, endeavor to assist the victim with whatever help she needs. Often, this means providing the victim with medical care as well as legal and psychological counseling. As well, the assailant should be disciplined for his criminal misconduct. At the very least, this might mean his removal from the residence hall or the college as a whole. If the victim wishes to file criminal charges against her assailant, the college administrative and counseling staff may wish to actively assist her in doing so.

Readers who may wish to familiarize themselves with the legal responsibilities of educational institutions to deal with sexual crimes are advised to consult the Sexual Assault Victims Bill of Rights (20 U.S.C. 1092 [f] [7]).

COPING WITH SELF-DESTRUCTIVE STUDENTS

The matter of dealing with suicidal and anorectic students will be discussed extensively in Chapter V. Therefore this subject, as it pertains to the residence hall, will be dealt with only briefly in this section.

Obviously, students who are observed to be behaving in a highly self-destructive manner (e.g., starving, mutilating themselves, threatening suicide) need immediate professional help. RAs should be trained to recognize the signs of the self-destructive behavior that many students conceal within the privacy of their own dormitory rooms. They can be instructed and encouraged to report incidents of self-destructive behavior and assisted in understanding the causes and effective methods for helping those who behave self-destructively.

In assisting the self-destructive student, RAs and administrators alike should be aware of the strong resistances some of these students display when offered help. These resistances may induce in the RA feelings of guilt and helplessness. At times the RA may become frustrated with the self-destructive student who refuses to receive professional help and reacts with inappropriate anger and disapproval. Clearly, they will need timely and sympathetic support from their administrative supervisors in dealing with intractably self-destructive students.

The dangerously self-destructive student deserves and requires immediate psychological and medical assistance, possibly including hospitalization. If such services are available on the campus itself, the college may be the primary resource of professional help. However, some colleges do not have a sufficient range of professional services with which to deal adequately with highly self-destructive students and therefore may need to rely upon off-campus community resources in order to deal with urgent situations. When faced with such situations, RAs and their supervisors should be intimately familiar with the agencies and services of their local communities to which they can immediately refer or transfer students who become dangerously self-destructive.

In dealing with highly self-destructive students in the residence hall it is important that RAs recognize the fact that such students not only endanger themselves but usually also adversely affect other students in the residence hall. Their self-destructive proclivities often cause other students to feel apprehensive, guilty and responsible for their ultimate safety and welfare.

The time and energy students sometimes devote to rescuing and succoring the suicidal student can have a decidedly debilitative effect upon themselves and lead to their own emotional difficulties. For this reason, RAs should be trained to help students who are coping with a self-destructive peer by first sympathizing with their plight but also pointing out that it is generally in no one's interest for students persistently to shoulder the primary responsibility for caring for a suicidal dorm mate. Students, therefore, must be encouraged by RAs to report incidents of self-destructive behavior in the dorm (anonymously, if necessary) and then offered counseling services if the crisis has caused a serious emotional upheaval in their own lives.

RAs also need to recognize that the potential harmful effects that a seriously self-destructive student can have upon other students may serve as grounds to discipline the student who persists in behaving dangerously, refuses professional help, and is indifferent and cavalier toward the harm that his or her behavior is causing others. RAs should be helped to understand that highly self-destructive behavior can also constitute socially disruptive behavior that is in violation of the student code of conduct and therefore must be reported, not just as a psychological or medical emergency, but also as a possible disciplinary matter.

Furthermore, the highly self-destructive students themselves should of course be informed by residential staff that their behavior is not only self-endangering but is disruptive to others and therefore may be subject to disciplinary procedures should it continue.

ASSAULTS, THEFTS, AND VANDALISM

Physical assaults, thefts, and vandalism are, unfortunately, commonplace in college residence halls throughout the country. Because of their frequency and ubiquity, residential staff all too frequently wink at and under-report these anti-social acts. Although one must not expect RAs to transform the residence hall into a police state in which all forms of anti-social behavior will be closely monitored and proscribed, there is much that can be done to deal with the problem of fighting, thievery and vandalism in dormitories.

First, using the carrot, residential staff can regularly meet with students to promote a positive, nurturing atmosphere toward personal relationships in the dorm. In these meetings, RAs can discuss the need for students to respect the personal and property rights of others. These meetings can be used to instill important social values regarding the need for all students to support, assist and respect one another in a common living situation. In these meetings, students can be helped to understand that they will not be expected to accept or tolerate acts of assault or abuse. They can be encouraged to report such acts by receiving assurances that their reports will be duly and conscientiously investigated with the purpose of redressing justifiable grievances.

Next, using the stick, RAs may need to remind students periodically that acts of assault, theft, or vandalism are serious violations of the code of student conduct and therefore will not be tolerated. Students should be told that, depending upon the repetitiveness and gravity of such anti-social acts, a student who is found guilty of such charges could suffer expulsion from the dormitory or even from the college. A set of less severe sanctions, such as mandatory reparations for acts of vandalism or proportionate restitution where one has been found guilty of assault or theft, can be instituted and publicized at the outset of each academic year, so that residence students fully understand the disciplinary implications of certain anti-social behavior.

It is generally in everyone's interest that colleges have a policy that prohibits firearms or other lethal weapons on campus. Students who, for whatever reason, are found with firearms in their possession should be dealt with immediately and decisively.

In a recent incident that occurred on a college campus in Massachusetts a student went on a shooting spree, killing two persons and wounding four others. Shortly before this rampage, the student had received a box in the mail from a company that supplied firearms. College officials, who by chance discovered whence the box was mailed, were justifiably suspicious and seriously considered confiscating and inspecting it. However, after a lengthy consultation with residence staff, they decided not to intercept the package. Instead, they later (evidently after the package had already been opened and ammunition had been removed) spoke with the student, who reopened the package and simply displayed rifle parts which he claimed were to be given to his father as a gift. He, naturally, denied lethal intent. Shortly afterward, he traveled to another city, purchased a semi-automatic assault rifle, returned to the campus, and carried out his plan of mayhem.

If packages arrive in residence halls that appear to contain dangerous weapons or explosives, college officials may be understandably reluctant to inspect those deliveries themselves, for fear of violating federal laws that safeguard the unintercepted delivery of mail. However, colleges certainly have a right to request that police or FBI agents come to the campus in order properly to evaluate whether such packages contain dangerous items and need to be removed immediately from the campus for the protection of the college as a whole.

Short of taking this particularly firm measure, if residence staff believe that a package from, say, a firearms manufacturer or supplier contains a lethal weapon, they may wish to impound the package temporarily, then take it to its intended recipient, and request that it be opened immediately in order that it's contents can be fully inspected for their potential lethality.

After all, if a gun manufacturer mails a heavy package to a residence hall, it is certainly not naive or foolish for residence staff to believe that the package might contain a dangerous weapon. If it does, and it is discovered that the student has solicited and willingly received that weapon on the college campus, he or she is clearly in serious violation of the code of student conduct and subject to disciplinary procedures. In any case, the package should be confiscated and impounded immediately, to be turned over to the appropriate law enforcement authorities as soon as possible.

DEALING WITH VARIOUS FORMS OF HARASSMENT

Harassment takes root and eventually raises its ugly head in an infinite number of ways. The contemporary American student lives in a racist society that tends to breed ethnic, religious, gender, and racial divisions, inequities, and intense enmities. It is not surprising, therefore, that the residence hall, which is often a melting pot of numerous subcultures, races and social classes, can spawn cultural and racial conflict that sometimes leads to the harassment and persecution of certain targeted groups of individuals.

Of course, considering all the many social, political, and economic factors that militate against forming a solidarity of diverse cultures and races in today's society, it is hardly realistic to think that college staff can, by themselves, completely eliminate racial discrimination and conflict within the culturally diverse milieu of a college dormitory. Yet, there is much that can be done to foster and enhance personal awareness and mutual respect for cultural and racial differences between students.

As a basic statement of policy and philosophy, the residence staff should establish beyond the shadow of a doubt that it stands firmly behind the principle of appreciating, understanding, respecting and accepting individual differences regardless of physical abilities, race, ethnicity, sexual orientation, religion, age, gender or political affiliation. This principle can and should be a moral guidepost for staff and students alike as they attempt to grapple with the challenge of cultural and racial diversity in the residence hall.

It can also serve as a moral underpinning for those activities and programs that serve to promote social and cultural awareness. Such activities and programs could, for example, include:

a. Providing personal outreach and support for individual students who are members of targeted groups.
b. Providing diverse social, cultural and recreational activities that address the specific needs of target group members.
c. Providing opportunities for leadership development for members of the target groups.
d. Providing training opportunities for residence staff and students that can increase their appreciation and acceptance of differences.
e. Confronting with judicial impartiality, firmness and moral courage, incidents that undermine the formation of a positive multicultural environment.
f. Providing significant and positive role models in professional and student positions as representatives of target groups.
g. Encouraging and supporting residential student organizations that will address the needs of underrepresented and targeted groups of students.
h. Funding and supporting a hotline for students such as gay and lesbian students who may find it difficult to "go public" with their personal problems, .
i. Co-sponsoring and providing financial support for selected college events that enhance awareness of and respect for cultural and racial diversity.

Finally, the college residence staff should provide effective opportunities for redress for those students who have been the targets of racial or cultural intolerance.

The author wishes to thank Mr. Chuck Rhodes, Dean of Student Housing, Sonoma State University and Ms. Laurie Amada, former RA, San Francisco State University, for their generous assistance with this chapter.

Chapter VI

The Role of the College Mental Health Program

The findings presented in this book are based upon clinical experience over the past twenty years in the City College of San Francisco Mental Health Program. The Mental Health Program (MHP) is an on-campus psychological service which provides short-term (i.e., 10-12 sessions) psychotherapy to community college students.

City College, like other urban community colleges, has a student population which reflects the diversity of the city itself. More than one-half of the students are from ethnic minorities. The majority of the students are between the ages of 18 and 29, an age group particularly susceptible to a variety of medical, social, and personal problems including venereal disease, substance abuse, and unwanted pregnancy.

THE INCREASING NUMBERS OF DISRUPTIVE COLLEGE STUDENTS

Over the last several years, college personnel throughout the nation have found themselves faced with an increasing number of disruptive students. Many disruptive incidents (fighting, alcohol and drug abuse, plagiarism, and date rape) appear to involve students who are quite diverse diagnostically. There is little doubt, however, that a significant number of the disruptive incidents reported by college employees involve students with such serious psychological disabilities as manic depression and schizophrenia, as well as some of the serious character disorders, particularly the antisocial personality (the sociopath) and the (acting out) borderline personality.

Several explanations have been advanced to account for the large increase in the numbers of seriously emotionally disturbed students attending colleges: legislative changes that have helped to retain and treat psychiatric patients in their local communities; advances in the use of psychotropic medications to stabilize psychiatric patients in local, noninstitutional settings; and the well-structured, culturally rich and hospitable qualities of the college campus itself, which are surely inviting to most students, including those with psychological disabilities.

In my contacts with college and university employees throughout the country, I have noted an appreciable increase in complaints that, as the community mental health system over the past decade or so has deteriorated as a result of severe funding cutbacks, larger numbers of seriously disturbed individuals are being admitted to colleges, especially community colleges. Many of these students are not receiving or, in many instances, even asking for, the full benefit of the local psychological and social services they desperately need if they are to succeed.

The MHP, which was established as a part of the Student Health Service in 1970, set forth several service priorities:

1. To deal effectively and rapidly with basically well functioning students in psychological crisis.
2. To refer those students in need of services that were not available at the college to other community resources.
3. To provide emergency services to those students who were gravely psychologically disabled or who were a danger to themselves or others, including procedures for hospitalizing such students, if necessary.
4. To provide educational "outreach services" (e.g., guest lectures, workshops) to the campus community that would assist staff and students to learn as much as possible about the maintenance of mental health.
5. To make consultation services readily available to all college personnel relative to their concerns about dealing with problematic students.

(Amada, 1983)

In order to implement these service goals, the following guidelines and policies were adopted: there would be no charges for services and intake was to be entirely voluntary; that is, no student would be seen against his or her wishes. All information was to be held in strict confidence within the Student Health Services, kept separate from all other student records. The importance of the preservation of confidentiality applied also to the question of whether or not a particular student had come to the clinic at all. The program would maintain an "open" intake, seeing any regularly enrolled student who applied as soon as possible after application. Waiting periods and waiting lists would be kept to a minimum (Amada, 1985).

Although the mainstay of the MHP has always been short-term, crisis-oriented psychotherapy, an increasingly important component of the program has been its consultation services to staff who have raised questions and complaints about the disruptive behavior of students. The role of the mental health consultant, because of its increasing importance to the college, has been carefully reviewed and refined since the inception of the MHP in order to maximize its effectiveness and value to the campus community. For understandable reasons, this role has sometimes been viewed in a controversial light.

Szasz (1973) stated that college psychotherapists are duplicitous and ineffectual in handling disruptive students because they are in actuality a "double agent," serving both administrators and students, but owing real loyalty to neither.

Blain and McArthur (1961) declared that, in dealing with the disruptive student, the college psychotherapist should not have any authority for discipline but instead should play an important role in delivering professional opinions regarding a student's personality in order to assist the institution in making the correct disposition of a disruptive incident.

Pavela (1982) pointed out that the role of the college mental health professional is severely limited in handling cases involving discipline because college therapists cannot adequately fulfill an expectation that they can determine which students experiencing "emotional problems" will actually engage in violent behavior.

The rapid and judicious resolution of disruptive behavior is often impeded or undermined by the very nature of the disruption itself. Orleans and Steimer (1984) suggested that very difficult human judgments are at stake in such instances. In their view, too severe a view of the situation may unfairly penalize the student; reluctance to make a judgment (or follow well-grounded intuition) may yield disaster.

Before describing how the role of the mental health consultant is carried out in cases involving disruptive students, it is perhaps best to explain the rationales for employing this particular role, rather than acceding to the requests of college personnel that campus psychotherapists undertake psychotherapy on an involuntary basis with disruptive students.

MANDATORY PSYCHOTHERAPY AS A FORM OF DISCIPLINE

Requiring Disruptive Students To Receive Psychotherapy

Requiring disruptive students to receive psychotherapy distorts and undermines the basis for corrective disciplinary action. The focus and impetus for disciplinary action is the disruptive behavior of the student, not the student's putative mental illness or disorder. When college administrators require the disruptive student to undertake psychotherapy, they are perforce making a *psychiatric* judgment using *psychiatric* criteria. Even if they were doing this with the benefit of having first consulted a mental health professional, the requirement is being carried out by means of the administrator's authority and, therefore, it is the administrator who is making the psychiatric determination that the student requires therapy. College administrators generally do not possess the legal right to make psychiatric evaluations and determinations of this nature. On the other hand, they most certainly do have the legal right and prerogative to determine what is and is not acceptable student behavior on their respective campuses and to carry out nonpsychiatric discipline in cases of student misconduct.

Motivations for Requiring Psychotherapy

The requirement of psychotherapy for the disruptive student is often motivated by fanciful and naive notions about psychotherapy itself. One such notion, for example, is the belief that once students receive psychotherapy, their disruptive behavior will abate or cease. Although this is sometimes true, it is also true that many persons who receive psychotherapy remain socially disruptive and at times actually become violent, despite their psychiatric treatment.

An analogous belief is that psychotherapists have the omnipotence not only to prevent disruptive behavior, but to accurately predict disruptive recidivism. Numerous research studies as well as common sense indicate that the ability of the mental health professional to predict some—especially violent—forms of disruptive behavior is admittedly quite limited. Monahan (1981), for example, cited five studies which capably demonstrated that clinical predictions of violent behavior among institutionalized mentally disordered people are accurate at best about one-third of the time. He further quotes the American Civil Liberties Union (ACLU) which has expressed a very dim (and, in my opinion, extremist) view of the lack of predictive prowess among mental health professionals.

The ACLU has flatly stated that "it now seems beyond dispute that mental health professionals have no expertise in predicting future dangerous behavior to self or others. In fact, predictions of dangerous behavior are wrong about 95% of the time" (Monahan, 1981, p. 28). In the next chapter there will be a discussion of some distinctions that can be made between predicting dangerous behavior and predicting nondangerous disruptive behavior. Suffice to say here, that although a mental health professional's ability to predict future disruptiveness is not omnisciently perfect, it is not, in my view, absolutely flawed to the extent that the ACLU has alleged.

There are at least two reasons why mental health professionals will be limited in predicting the disruptive behavior of students:

1. The way in which psychiatric patients think and behave in the consultation room often has little relationship or carry-over to how they will behave and think elsewhere. Thus, therapists, especially if they do not understand well their patients' states of mind, may have an unrealistic view of their social functioning and their potential for behaving disruptively outside the consultation room.

2. No psychotherapist, no matter how sensitive or astute, can anticipate the myriad stressful circumstances which a patient may en-

counter on the college campus. Thus, patients may be well fortified by their therapy to enter college; however, once there, a poor grade, a humiliating academic evaluation, or a long delay on the registration line can cause the emotionally fragile student to regress and become disruptive.

For these reasons, the common practice of requiring psychiatric agencies and practitioners to submit reports to administrators indicating their patients' readiness to re-enroll is suspect and should be, in my view, abolished. In the next chapter I will describe an alternative procedure that I believe is far more appropriate and useful in dealing with reenrolling students who have been suspended from the campus for disruptive behavior.

Another fanciful notion that sometimes motivates college staff to favor mandatory psychotherapy for disruptive students is the assumption that such students have obviously never before received such help and should now, for the first time, avail themselves of the golden opportunity afforded them by a free and convenient psychological service on the campus. Oftentimes, this assumption is made because the staff member—who thinks of psychotherapy as a treatment with a permanently civilizing effect—finds it impossible to believe that a student who has behaved outrageously could have ever been a recipient of a course of psychotherapy. Yet, quite often I have discovered that many of the students who have been reported by faculty for being disruptive had actually been clients of the college MHP and, as well, were prior long-term patients of other psychiatric agencies in the community (a fact that, for reasons of confidentiality, could not be disclosed to complainants).

Required Psychotherapy as a Coercive Measure

Requiring a disruptive student to receive psychotherapy is unequivocally a coercive measure that serves to instill in the student resentment toward the therapist and therapy. If such students conform to this requirement, and on many campuses they do, they will agree to see a therapist but frequently will make no personal investment in the treatment process itself. As a consequence, such students typically derive little from the therapy other than the impression that psychotherapy is a form of punishment that must be stoically endured.

Confidentiality in Psychotherapy

For psychotherapy to work effectively, it must ordinarily be conducted on a confidential basis. Requiring a disruptive student to receive psychotherapy often removes this cornerstone of therapy because someone, either the student or the therapist, will eventually be expected to report to the college administration that the student is, indeed, receiving psychotherapeutic services.

Several safeguards can generally serve to protect confidentiality in such cases.
a. Therapists may refuse to transmit substantive reports about students who have not given their voluntary, written consent to this procedure.
b. Students who have been referred for psychotherapy may willingly and, in writing, authorize their therapists to transmit certain information about themselves to specified college officials.
c. Students who are referred to therapists may be permitted explicitly to refuse, for whatever reason, the disclosure of therapists' reports about themselves to college officials without the threat of duress, penalty, or reprisal on the part of the college. In this regard, it is probably worth mentioning that there are differences of opinion among both mental health professionals and college administrators regarding what constitutes "substantive" disclosures that violate the confidentiality of students who receive psychotherapy.

In my own view, the simple fact that a student has entered psychotherapy is intrinsically substantive (and potentially inflammatory) information that should not be disclosed without the express voluntary and written consent of the student himself or herself. Although the disclosure of such limited information may seem quite innocuous, it can be used by the college, with or without intention, to embarrass, stigmatize, or manipulate students. I believe, therefore, that the student's decision to enter therapy should be given the same protections of confidentiality as are accorded the personal self-disclosures that later follow during the psychotherapy sessions themselves.

Required Psychotherapy as a Transfer of Authority

As suggested earlier, the administrative requirement of psychotherapy tends to transfer the responsibility and authority for administering discipline from where it rightfully belongs—the office of the designated administrator—to where it does not belong—the offices of counselors and therapists.

Required Psychotherapy and Section 504

The requirement that disruptive students receive psychotherapy as a condition of continued enrollment is essentially predicated upon a policy that can exclude them because of their alleged mental or psychiatric disability. This is probably in violation of Section 504 of the Rehabilitation Act of 1973, which reads, in part: "No otherwise qualified handicapped individual shall, solely by reasons of his handicap, be excluded from participation in, be denied the benefits of, or be subjected to discrimination under any program or activity receiving Federal financial assistance."

In other words, the antiquated practice of requiring disruptive students to receive psychological evaluations and/or psychotherapy is forcing these students to define themselves as persons who have a psychological disability. Considering the many schools that still resort to its use and abuse (the prevailing attitude seems to be, "I'll do it this way as long as I can get away with it."), it is truly extraordinary that college attorneys do not spend more time in courts defending those schools that regularly engage in this questionable practice.

Some college psychotherapists and counselors undertake mandatory or coercive psychotherapy with students even when they have ethical objections to this practice. Quite frequently, referrals for mandatory counseling or psychotherapy are made by an administrator who exercises some form of administrative authority and control over the mental health or counseling program. When this administrator authoritatively insists that students be seen for psychotherapy, college psychotherapists who refuse to comply with such requests may be placing themselves and their programs in jeopardy.

Conceivably, refusal to fulfill such requests may come back to haunt college psychotherapists or counselors in the form of funding cutbacks or unfriendly administrative policies and rulings vis-a-vis their programs. In any event, just imagining such a prospect could very well be a sufficient deterrent to many college psychotherapists and counselors who have ethical qualms about mandatory referrals.

An analog to this dilemma that exists within the private sector applies to the role of private practitioners who accept mandatory referrals from colleges for psychological evaluations and treatment. Although these therapists, too, may have moral qualms about the legitimacy of this procedure, they may also realize that to refuse the college's request for such assistance may mean that they will cease to be used by the college as a community resource in the future. Obviously, it does not require an overabundance of venality on the part of private practitioners for them to disrelish and seek to avoid this unpleasant possibility. Thus, they may set aside their own ethical qualms about mandatory referrals from the college, at least for the time being.

In this regard, I have noticed that many therapists who are faced with this ethical quandary eventually transmit to colleges psychiatric reports that are so vague and so ambiguous as to be utterly indecipherable and of no practical value to the college. I suspect that many of these reports are deliberately written ambiguously, in part to assuage the guilt of the therapist for sending the report in the first place and also to minimize the potential harm the report eventually might cause the student in the college setting. Naturally, many college administrators who attempt to interpret and enlist these reports to carry out disciplinary decisions are frustrated and bewildered by them, perhaps without realizing that often they were written precisely to obfuscate the reader.

THE ROLE OF THE MENTAL HEALTH CONSULTANT

In cases in which reported disruptive students are considered acutely psychotic or a danger to themselves or others, the on-campus mental health team can facilitate the psychiatric hospitalization of the student in a timely, efficient, and humane manner.

In cases that involve disruptive students who do not pose such dangers, the mental health consultant can assist instructors and other college staff by offering emotional support and timely advice to them as they strive to resolve the disruptive crisis. Also, because instructors and administrators sometimes have widely different and conflicting viewpoints regarding the causes and the degree of the seriousness of disruptive crises, they may tend to favor and pursue disparate courses of action to resolve them. The mental health consultant can assist them by identifying areas of disagreement and, as a mediator for the contending principals, offer recommendations about how their differences and the crisis, itself, can best be resolved.

The following vignette is a composite of many consultative discussions I have had with instructors who have reported disruptive students to me. It is primarily used to illustrate how the role of the consultant is utilized in such situations.

A Discussion Regarding a Disruptive Student . . .

Maintaining Confidentiality

Instructor: Dr. Amada, I'd like to ask you about a student of mine. He's really been troubling me lately. It's his behavior. Perhaps you know him, Joe Smith?

Amada: Well, unfortunately, I can't, for reasons of confidentiality, tell you whether or not I know him. But I can probably help you anyway. So why don't you tell me some of your concerns.

Instructor: Well, I thought if you knew him, it would help. You see, I think he's got a mental problem or something. Maybe even a drug problem. Anyway, I think he needs help. So, I was wondering if I could just send him over to your department. Would you see him? Do you have time today, perhaps?

Amada: Well, before we decide what to do about this student, why don't you tell me what's been going on.

Identifying the Problem

Instructor: Where should I start? There seems to be so much to tell you.

Amada: Why don't you start by telling me, concretely and specifically, something about this student's behavior. What, exactly, he has been doing that upsets you.

Instructor: Well, he's been acting nuts. Wacko. That's what he's been doing. Could you tell me if he's possibly mentally ill?

Amada: Perhaps if you could just tell me what he's been doing in your class, I could suggest an effective means of handling this student. Let's just stick to the behavior you have been observing. What do you find objectionable or unacceptable about it? And how long has it been going on?

Instructor: Well, it all started several weeks ago when the student submitted a paper. I teach an English course and I asked the students to write a paper on the pros and cons of capital punishment. When I got Joe Smith's paper back, I was dumbfounded. I mean, it wasn't just written badly. It was filled with invective. Wild and ugly comments about how capital punishment should be used to kill off minority groups, gay people, welfare recipients. It was awful. I had never before read such hateful diatribe. It made me angry. You know, beside the convoluted and unintelligible writing, the man's ideas were abhorrent to me. I wanted to throw him the hell out of my class right then and there.

Amada: What happened next?

Instructor: Well, I failed him on the paper. I met with him in my office, where I informed him that I didn't appreciate his racist and ugly attacks, and, as his instructor, I judged the paper to be completely lacking in acceptable scholarship. Did I do the right thing?

Amada: Go on and tell me what happened next.

Instructor: He became nasty and angry with me. He told me he was entitled to his beliefs and, if I didn't like them, I was a bigot myself. He said that I couldn't hold his beliefs against him. He said that he wanted and deserved a passing grade. I told him that that was impossible because, aside from his objectionable ideas, his paper was unacceptable on scholarly grounds. He left the office in a huff.

Amada: What happened next?

Instructor: Well, the student remained in my class. But his behavior became more belligerent and disruptive.

Amada: In what way?

Instructor: Well, he began to challenge everything I said. He constantly interrupted my lectures by voicing opinions that were contrary to mine. This wasn't easy to deal with.

Amada: Why not?

Instructor: Because I normally encourage students to voice their opinions, even if they strongly disagree with mine.

Amada: But this was different, wasn't it?

Instructor: Yes, of course.

Amada: How?

Instructor: Well, it was more flagrant, more repetitive, and usually rather irrelevant to the subject under discussion.

Amada: How did you handle that?

Instructor: Well, at first, I just tried to tolerate and ignore it.

Amada: And how well did that work?

Instructor: It didn't. It got worse. Finally, I called him into my office again. I told him his disruptive behavior would have to stop. It was interfering with my ability to teach.

Amada: What did he say?

Instructor: He said I was picking on him and he would report me to the Dean.

Amada: Did he?

Instructor: I don't think so. But I don't know what to do. He's still in my class and he's still disrupting it. I really can't stand this much longer and the other students are also feeling upset about my inability to handle the situation. A few have already spoken about him to me and asked that I do something or they might quit the class. What should I do? Should I send him over to you so you could have a talk with him?

Amada: No. There's a better approach than that. Let me give you some guidelines and procedures for handling this situation.

Instructor: Good. That's just what I need. I'd appreciate it.

Guidance for Corrective Action

Amada: First, you should know that you, as an instructor, have two general prerogatives. The first, and most obvious, is your right to establish and enforce academic standards for students. You set the standards and you grade students accordingly. The second prerogative is your right to set behavioral standards within each class. Here, the idea is to set reasonable standards and expect reasonable conformity to those standards.

The principle to keep in mind is one of reasonable accommodation. In other words, small infractions, such as a student who chatters too loudly during a lecture, can be ignored or dealt with by a simple warning or admonition. Major infractions, however, such as when a student repeatedly and intractably interrupts lectures and disregards the instructor's attempts to curtail the behavior, should, of course, not be accommodated.

Now, I would say from your description of the student that you have already gone well beyond the point of having made reasonable accommodations to his behavior and that it is now time to take several steps.

Instructor: What are those?

Amada: Well, I know you have already warned the student about his behavior, but have you warned him in writing?

Instructor: No, I haven't. Should I?

Amada: Yes. Document your observations and expectations. Tell the student in writing in what respects he has behaved unacceptably. Check out the student code of conduct on this campus and you will see that this student is probably in violation of that code. The codes that specifically prohibit continued disruptive behavior and the persistent defiance of authority can be used. In writing up your report, document concretely those incidents that violate those codes. Don't editorialize or use psychological terms or jargon, and don't use psychological speculations about his alleged "mental condition." Stick to his behavior. Send a copy of your report to your chairperson and have him or her send a copy to the dean. Now, you have several options.

Instructor: What are those?

Developing Options and Procedural Steps

Amada: Well, after having warned the student about his behavior in writing, you can wait to see if that behavior recurs. If it does, you can then ask the dean to have the student removed from your class. Or, if you think that the situation is already untenable, and, by the way, I do, you can now ask the dean to intervene and see if he would be willing to remove the student from your class immediately. Chances are, he would call the student in, question him and then decide. It's possible, of course, that he might want more than retroactive documentation. He might just warn the student and give him another chance in your class. If you want the student out of your class now, say so in your report.

Now, another available option to you is to meet with the student again, or have the dean meet with him, in order to tell him that he is on his way to failing the course for academic reasons (which is no doubt true) and that in order for him to avoid the penalty of a failing grade, he should withdraw from the class now. If this is done in a calm, non-blaming and empathic manner, many students will accept this option without further ado. It might be worth a try.

Instructor: What's next?

Amada: Well, let's say the student is permitted to remain in your class. The first time he repeats his unacceptable behavior, you report that to the dean and request his removal. By the way, here in California you are permitted to remove the student yourself, unilaterally, for two consecutive classes. That measure sometimes helps to cool off a bad situation and buys time for the implementation of an administrative investigation.

Instructor: Anything else?

Amada: Yes. Let's take the worst scenario, just to cover all the bases. Let's say the student defies all of these interventions and persists in his disruptive behavior. If he does, don't confront him directly. If necessary, call the campus police and have him taken into custody. Do that also if he in any manner attempts to menace or threaten you, verbally or physically.

Instructor: (With some trepidation) Are you saying this because you think he's dangerous?

Amada: No. I doubt that he's dangerous. Most such students are not dangerous. However, no one, including mental health professionals, can predict with absolute certainty that a given student will not be violent. So, you need to take precautions. Don't endanger yourself or your other students by directly confronting or trying to control Mr. Smith.

Instructor: What happens if the Dean doesn't think he can remove him and he gets worse.

Assisting Resolution of Problem

Amada: That's what I'm discussing with you. In this case, mention in your report that you have consulted with me and that I have recommended an immediate evaluation of this matter and that, in my estimation, the student's removal from your class seems advisable at this time. If that doesn't work, let me know and I will contact the Dean myself and see if I can expedite this matter. I might, if it's O.K. with you, contact the Dean anyway in order to prepare him for the submission of your report. He might appreciate that.

Instructor: Sure, go ahead. Anything else?

Amada: Yes. At any place in this process where you feel you need further assistance, don't hesitate to call me. Do something about this situation now so that it doesn't get worse. I'm here to help you with this.

Instructor: But doesn't this guy need help? As angry as I am with him, I think he's sad. He could sure use some counseling. Don't you want to see him anyway?

Amada: No, I don't think so. Under the circumstances, I don't think that would be especially helpful. Of course, if in your conversation with him he indicates that he wants psychological help, you can refer him. But if you do, you must make it clear to him that whether he receives our help or not, his disruptive behavior must stop and that seeing a therapist won't get him off that hook.

Instructor: So, is he crazy? Schizophrenic?

Amada: As I've said, it's really best to keep a student's diagnosis out of this. That's, at best, speculative anyway and only tends to confuse matters. It's his behavior that matters, not his so-called psychiatric condition.

Instructor: I think I'm beginning to get it. I can't discipline this guy for his mental condition, but I can for his disruptive behavior.

Amada: You've got it.

Guidance in Responding to Incidents

Instructor: Can I ask you a couple of more questions?

Amada: Sure.

Instructor: What about his paper. I jumped on him about his ideas and then about his incompetent writing. I couldn't help it, he was so hateful. Was that a good thing to do or not?

Amada: Probably not. Since the paper was basically a test of his writing skills and not his ideas, it probably would have been best to evaluate only the scholarly aspects of his writing. Since the paper was atrociously written, it would have been sufficient to grade it solely on narrow academic grounds, rather than challenge his prejudices, however abhorrent they are to you and me. To challenge his bigoted views gave him leverage to switch the focus away from where it belonged. Namely, that he had done a terrible job of writing the paper and deserved a failing grade, not for his ideas, but for the poor quality of his writing.

Instructor: I'm glad that you clarified that. Because I knew I was getting off the point somewhere and couldn't quite figure out what to do about it. That's helpful. One more question?

Amada: Sure. Shoot.

Instructor: I didn't mention this earlier, but when I first had trouble with this student, I tried to be helpful and reassuring by patting him on the shoulder during one of our office interviews. He seemed uneasy with this. Was this a mistake?

Amada: Probably. Most students seem to appreciate a friendly pat on the back from an instructor now and then. However, there are some hypersensitive students who find it difficult to tolerate those kind of friendly gestures. They sometimes misinterpret them and are apt to thereafter regard the instructor as more a friend than a professional who exercises institutional authority such as the power to grade papers. So, I would suggest that in the future, before touching a student, that you feel confident that you know that student well enough to know that the pat on the back will not be badly misinterpreted.

Instructor: Thanks a lot. Can I get back to you if I need to?

Amada: By all means. Let me know how it goes, one way or another.

Chapter VII

Some Special Problems

DISRUPTIVENESS VERSUS DANGEROUSNESS

The relative inability of psychotherapists to predict dangerousness is an important fact for lay and professional persons to recognize so that they can deal effectively and realistically with individuals who pose the risk of manifesting violent behavior. Nevertheless, this acknowledgment has only sporadic and peripheral relevance to most cases of disruptive student behavior. Specifically, if the prediction of dangerousness is at best precarious, the prediction of many forms of nondangerous but highly *disruptive* behavior on the college campus is not nearly so fraught with the risk of error, bias, or injustice. Most disruptive behavior that is ultimately reported to the administration by college personnel is blatant, publicly observable, and highly recurrent.

Because disruptive behavior that has already become chronic, flagrant, and publicly offensive ordinarily instigates an instructor to report the student, it is usually not inordinately difficult for an administrator to predict rather accurately whether the disruptive behavior will continue unabated without the intervention of discipline. For example, only common sense and logic would be necessary to predict that a student who, week after week, has been interrupting lectures with loud and raucous catcalls is, in all likelihood, going to continue doing so if he or she is not disciplined for this behavior. It should always be borne in mind, however, that even the best predictions and most ingenious uses of discipline will not necessarily alter or rein in the disruptive behavior of some highly intractable students.

The potential for violence on the college campus is far more difficult to predict than the potential for nonviolent forms of disruptiveness for several reasons:

1. With some exceptions, violent acts of disruption committed by students fortunately tend to occur less frequently and are less likely

to fall into a pattern than other, more innocuous, forms of disruption. Observable patterns of behavior, by their very nature, lend themselves to prediction far better than more sporadic forms of behavior.
2. In contrast to many nonviolent disruptive acts on college campuses, most genuinely violent behavior—murder, rape, arson, or assault and battery—is carried out stealthily, often concealed behind closed doors, and, for lack of witnesses, shielded from detection. Moreover, the locus of past violent crimes is likely to have been in the off-campus community, not on the college campus itself. Therefore, even if the perpetrator had been prosecuted and convicted of a prior violent crime, it is unlikely that the college would be privy to this violent history. Of course, if the institution did learn of the history, appropriate records relating to any criminal conviction could be obtained from the court that handled the matter, as adult crime records are public records that are always open to the public.

In short, because prior patterns of violent behavior tend to be more sporadic and far less ascertainable than most patterns of nonviolent disruptive behavior—especially in those cases reported by college staff precisely because they have become chronic and public nuisances—violence and dangerousness are ordinarily much more difficult to predict than nondangerous disruptive behavior.

In sum, the conflation of the terms *dangerousness* and *disruptiveness* is unfortunate and often misleading when applied to disruptive college students' behavior. Although dangerousness remains elusively unpredictable, most reported cases of student disruptiveness, given their generally recidivous and flagrant nature, lend themselves to fairly accurate predictions of future disruptiveness.

MENTAL ILLNESS AND DANGEROUSNESS

Many studies have commendably demonstrated that mental illness is not synonymous with either dangerousness or criminality (Phillips, Wolf, and Coon, 1988; Steadman, 1983; Teplin, 1985). These studies help to debunk and dispel public myths and prejudices about the mentally ill and are therefore of immense general importance. Yet, in assessing most college student disruptive behavior in particular, these studies are of limited value.

According to countless reports I and other mental health professionals have received from campuses across the United States and Canada, many, if not most, incidents of serious disruption—save perhaps alcohol and drug abuse, plagiarism, date rape, and fighting (serious forms of disruption that seem to involve students who are quite diverse diagnostically)—appear to involve students with serious psychological disabilities.

Although these diverse reports are anecdotal, impressionistic, and imprecise, they quite often suggest that the highly disruptive student is also, psychologically, a rather seriously disturbed individual. Particularly suggestive is the recurrent plaint one commonly hears or reads in these reports: The offending student is acting in a demonstrably bizarre manner, and the student's behavior seems inspired by hallucinatory, delusional, or paranoiac psychological processes. When school authorities have been able to procure such information from these students or their families, an extensive history of severe psychological difficulties and even psychiatric hospitalization is often revealed.

Such factors represent some of the generally reliable hallmarks of mental illness. Nevertheless, the contention that there is a high correlation between mental illness and many forms of on-campus disruptiveness remains largely inferential and, therefore, unproved and controversial at this time. Because of the paucity of good research studies in this area, our understanding of this problem remains murky. Future research studies, it is hoped, will be able to shed better light on the relationship between student disruptiveness and mental illness.

The importance of this point is obviously not to stigmatize or establish the moral culpability of the disruptive or mentally ill student. Rather, it is to underscore one of the major points of this book: If it is fair and accurate to assume that significant numbers of disruptive incidents actually involve students with psychological disabilities, the simple, humanitarian values to which our colleges are avowedly committed should inspire them to develop effective and comprehensive programs for psychologically disabled students that integrate them better into the educational community and reduce their potential for manifesting disruptive behavior. One example of such a program would be an on-campus mental health service that would provide treatment to the psychologically disabled student (and, presumably, to all other students) on a voluntary basis and in the early phases of a potentially disruptive crisis.

Although not all potentially disruptive students would use such a service, an appreciable number undoubtedly would, thereby reducing the overall number of disruptive incidents on campus. A programmatic approach of this kind is certainly preferable to a plan that resorts to mandatory referrals for psychological treatment *after* a student has become disruptive.

Psychological services that are provided to disruption-prone students on a voluntary basis and at a time when the students have not already committed acts of disruption have a decided advantage. Generally, students who enter psychotherapy on their own volition, rather than as a result of a mandatory disciplinary process, are more highly motivated to make positive use of their psychotherapeutic experience and will therefore be less likely to manifest disruptive behavior.

THE USE OF MANDATORY PSYCHIATRIC WITHDRAWALS

It is generally recommended that colleges avoid using "psychiatric" or "medical" withdrawals in order to suspend, expel, or simply remove disruptive students from their campuses. The use of a psychiatric withdrawal will probably require a (possibly involuntary) psychiatric evaluation and diagnosis, a measure that may not withstand legal scrutiny and challenge, partly because of the possibly coercive and involuntary nature of the evaluative procedure itself, and partly because of the imprecise and ambiguous nature of many such diagnoses.

At the risk of appearing to contradict myself, I should indicate that I regard the formulation and use of psychiatric diagnoses as highly useful guideposts in my own clinical practice. I would, however, argue that these same diagnoses, even when formulated and propounded by renowned authorities in the mental health field, should not be used for punitive or disciplinary purposes such as removing students from college. In addition to the questionable legality of such procedures, their enlistment in the context of carrying out disciplinary measures bastardizes, in my view, the primary and unassailable purpose and value of developing a diagnostic nosology in the first place—to improve psychotherapeutic treatment.

In addition to the possibility of inadvertently stigmatizing students with invidious labeling, the (mis)use of psychiatric diagnoses to effect withdrawals of disruptive students serves to undermine the college's efforts to impose just and proportionate discipline. The college has the legal right, assuming that due process has been followed and the student's constitutional rights have been adequately protected, to suspend or expel a student who has been seriously disruptive—for that student's *behavior*. It should not, and need not, try to adduce superfluous, legally questionable, psychiatric rationales for removing the disruptive student from the campus, especially since these selfsame rationales may ultimately be used in later judicial proceedings by the disruptive student to challenge effectively the propriety of an expulsion based upon psychiatric criteria.

My point is not to impugn the diagnostic skills of psychiatrists and psychologists but, rather, to caution against using psychiatric evaluations and diagnostic criteria, regardless of their scientific accuracy and validity, to carry out a procedure that is essentially disciplinary. As Steele has pointed out, "Colleges and universities considering any attempts to subject the mentally handicapped to mandatory psychiatric withdrawal should seek legal advice" (1984, pg. 341).

Pavela (1985) has suggested that mandatory psychiatric withdrawals might have possible use to remove from campus students who are suicidal or seriously anorectic. He also cautions that such practices not be adopted as policy because suicidal or anorectic persons are not necessarily "mentally ill." My own recommendation is as follows: Students who are either suicidal or suffer from severe anorexia should be immediately helped to receive in- or out-patient psychological and medical services as regularly and intensively as necessary. If the students' life-threatening behaviors persist, with or without the benefit of treatment, they should be regarded as disruptive conduct because the students' persistent self-imperiling behaviors are eventually likely to traumatize and victimize others—roommates, classmates, and the college personnel who must deal with them throughout each crisis.

For example, the roommates of recurrently suicidal students sometimes engage in protracted and abortive rescue efforts that, in time, snuff out their ability to sustain academic work and can lead to their own scholastic failure and withdrawal from college. College authorities must consider the welfare of these students, as well, when dealing with the highly self-destructive student.

In my view, the college can justifiably impose a suspension or expulsion strictly based on the student's disruptive behavior, without resorting to the use of psychiatric diagnoses, if the following three conditions can be met:

1. the persistent self-destructive behavior of the suicidal or anorectic student is having a markedly deleterious effect upon other students and/or staff;
2. disciplinary sanctions have already been imposed upon the suicidal or anorectic student for the harm that has been inflicted upon others;
3. the suicidal or anorectic student flouts the disciplinary sanctions by continuing to pursue his or her self-destructive courses of action.

In brief, the suicidal or seriously anorectic student can be removed from the campus for repeatedly behaving in a manner that is dangerous to self and others, not because he or she suffers from a mental illness. If, however, the college believes it is in the student's interest to withdraw immediately but, for humanitarian reasons, does not wish to impose disciplinary sanctions, it can offer the student the opportunity to leave with impunity. If the student accepts this offer and leaves, the college, rather than refer to the student's departure as a "psychiatric" or "medical" withdrawal, can simply call it a "withdrawal"—a term that is deliberately nebulous and nonstigmatizing.

Lest I be considered callous and indifferent to the suffering of suicidal or anorectic students, I think it apt to point out a common characteristic of these students. Quite frequently such students will rigidly refuse to enter psychotherapy or medical treatment to deal with their life-threatening behavior. Often, they display a gross indifference, contempt, or egocentricity toward the emotional rights and needs of those persons who may suffer acutely from being regularly exposed to their self-destructive behavior. Attempts by therapists to help them are often met by denial and pertinacity. The use of discipline, perhaps in the form of a suspension or expulsion, may be necessary in cases in which psychological and medical assistance have failed. Such discipline is not used to punish, but possibly to save a human life and to protect the emotional rights of those who must continually and inescapably witness the dangerous behavior of highly self-abusive individuals.

Before concluding, it may also be helpful to mention that those college staff who are responsible for dealing with the psychological and medical needs of students must be prepared to expedite the immediate hospitalization, perhaps on an involuntary basis, of students who are dangerously suicidal or anorectic. Situations in which there is a duty to warn on the part of psychotherapists—if necessary, without a client's permission—because a client poses a serious threat to someone else, are legally governed by the parameters of the case that has come to be known as the Tarasoff Decision (*Tarasoff v. Regents of the University of California*, 17 Cal.3d 425). The general legal requirements for psychotherapists in regard to the *Tarasoff* warning are as follows:

1. Under state civil codes the duty to warn must be based upon a communication from the patient to the therapist of a threat of physical violence, the threat must be a serious one, and the intended victim or victims must be reasonably identifiable. In order to discharge the duty to warn and protect under the circumstances specified above, the psychotherapist must make reasonable efforts to communicate the threat to the intended victim or victims or others likely to apprise the intended victim or victims and must notify a law enforcement agency.

2. The California Supreme Court, in adjudicating the *Tarasoff* case, ruled that, relative to Evidence Code Section 1014 (patient-psychotherapist privilege), public policy favoring protection of the confidential character of patient-psychotherapist communications must yield to the extent to which disclosure is essential to avert danger to others. This means that when the danger of violence to another person exists, the therapist has a responsibility to act as a private citizen. As a private citizen, a person of good conscience will not hesitate to warn an intended victim.

3. Psychotherapists must determine whether or not a breach of confidentiality under the welfare and institution codes of their state is warranted for a given situation. If the danger of violence to another specific person exists, then the obligation for the therapist to warn certainly outweighs any risk taken for breach of confidentiality.

4. Persons to be notified in a *Tarasoff* situation must include the intended victim, others who may apprise the intended victim of danger, and the police. The therapist must take all necessary steps to warn that are appropriate and proportionate to the circumstances. This could mean a telephone call, a personal visit, a telegram, or a letter. It is reasonable to provide the police with the name and address of the client who has made the threats. It is not normally permissible,

however, to provide the police with access to confidential patient records without a court order.
5. Given the gravity of such circumstances, serious consideration should ordinarily be given to initiating the hospitalization of the threatening client, involuntarily if necessary.

In certain states, education codes require that all employees of public educational institutions must report incidents that pose a serious danger to others, to their administrative supervisors and to the local enforcement authorities.

Finally, colleges will probably find it useful to develop policies and guidelines for referring students to mental health professionals expressly to secure evaluations that provide a perspective about the degree of illness, self-control, dangerousness, and potential suicidality of disruptive students. Such evaluations might enable administrators to deal more confidently and effectively with disruptive students.

My own recommendation regarding such policies is as follows: If a psychological or psychiatric evaluation is deemed helpful, the college should seek the student's voluntary, written consent for this procedure, including permission for the mental health professional to discuss the general findings of the evaluation with specified college officials. If the student refuses to undergo such an evaluation, his or her wishes must be respected and no penalty should be attached to this refusal. College administrators may feel that they are unduly foiled in carrying out an important duty by what appears to be an excessive adherence to the rules of confidentiality and the principle of self-determination, but it is important for all college personnel, including mental health professionals, to respect students' rights to refuse psychiatric examinations and treatment.

A single, but major, exception to this rule are those students who are demonstrably an imminent danger to themselves or others. Obviously these students must be examined on an involuntary basis and perhaps even hospitalized against their wishes.

I have found, in my consultations with administrators, that a member of the mental health staff can usually provide a useful perspective regarding the student's degree of self-control and readiness to conform to the codes of student conduct without actually interviewing the student. These perspectives are based upon careful interviews with the complainants and with the designated administrator to gain detailed descriptions of the disruptive student's behavior, from which quite reliable impressions and recommendations can be formulated by the mental health staff.

In handling matters strictly by consulting with the complainant and the designated administrator rather than by attempting to cajole the disruptive student to undergo a psychiatric examination, mental health professionals gain two decided advantages:
1. they are not bound by rules of confidentiality because they have neither treated nor examined the disruptive student, and therefore,

can speak quite freely about their impressions of the student, albeit on the basis of others' reports;
2. they do not have to contend with overly suspicious, resentful, and belligerent students who have a (perhaps quite realistic) notion that the data derived from the psychiatric examination ultimately will be used against them.

CONDITIONS OF RE-ENROLLMENT

Students who have been suspended or expelled for disciplinary reasons should be required to meet with the designated administrator if they wish to re-enroll. That administrator should spell out the conditions that the student must meet to return to the campus. If considered advantageous, they may be in the form of a written contract. Generally, the conditions should be that the student must adequately conform to the codes of student conduct of the college. If the student is not familiar with the codes, they should be produced and explained simply and specifically. If the student was originally suspended for a particular form of disruptive behavior, the administrator can remind the student that repetition of that behavior will probably result in additional and perhaps more severe disciplinary sanctions, including the possibility of yet another, more protracted suspension.

At one college I recently visited, students were interviewed and evaluated for re-enrollment by a panel consisting of a cross-section of the college staff. I learned about this panel because I was asked what the college should do about the many serious threats that were leveled at panel members by students who were denied readmission. As a result of these threats, panel members had become trepid and reluctant to complete their tenure on the panel. My advice was to indicate in the student codes that all threats made to members of the readmission committee would be regarded as seriously disruptive and punishable behavior.

Finally, two other recommendations for administrators are in order. *First,* because many disruptive students are disruptive often and in the presence of many different college personnel, it is possible that a single disruptive student will be reported to the appropriate administrator many times during the student's career at the college. It is advisable, therefore, that the administrator keep accurate records of each incident, including the names of the student and the complainant as well as a detailed description of the disruptive behavior. This will enable the administrator to discipline students who have engaged in multiple or ongoing acts of disruption on the basis of their cumulative (and, therefore, more serious) disruptive history, rather than treating each incident as isolated from all others (and, therefore, less seriously than they probably should).

Second, whether a reported disruptive incident has been administratively resolved or not, it is essential, as indicated earlier, that the designated administrator regularly apprise the complainant of the status of the investigation. Without the benefit of this information, the complainant is unnecessarily left to wonder and worry about whether the disruptive crisis will actually be resolved. Failure to follow this procedure will probably leave many administrators open to the criticism, warranted or not, that their failure to report their findings signifies that, alas, they have not done their job.

CONFLICTS OVER THE USE OF MEDICATIONS

It is quite common for college psychotherapists and administrators to become entangled in time-consuming and fruitless power struggles with disruptive students over the students' failure to use prescribed psychotropic medications. Frequently, in the course of advising or disciplining the disruptive student, it is discovered that the student is in psychiatric treatment and has been receiving a prescription from his or her therapist for medications. Because such students are manifesting disruptive behavior, it is often deemed advisable to question them about the regularity of their use of those medications. At this point, the discovery is sometimes made that these students have interrupted their use of the prescribed medications. This leads to the quite logical conclusion that it is this remissness on the students' part that is aggravating their psychiatric condition and causing them to be disruptive.

Even students who largely benefit from the use of prescribed medications may, from time to time, feel the need to abandon the drugs. For some students, the ongoing use of medications interferes with their sense of personal autonomy and is therefore a source of humiliation. For others, the side effects, both immediate (drowsiness) and potentially long-range (damage to internal organs), of the medications are a strong dissuasive factor. In some instances, students with paranoid disorders refuse to use prescribed medications because they consider them poisonous.

In my view, the therapists and administrators who engage in protracted disputes with such students are making an uncalled-for mistake. These professionals may spend many wasteful hours trying to convince students that it is in their best interest to resume the use of medications. Underlying their arguments is the highly plausible assumption that the medications will help to stabilize the student and thereby quell his or her disruptiveness. Yet, too often, these students adamantly refuse to yield to the logic of such arguments, leaving the college staff perplexed and stymied in their search for a solution to the problem.

I would suggest the following solution: First, realize that the student's use or disuse of medications is secondary to the central issue of whether the student is conforming to the codes of student conduct. Clearly, the student has the inviolable right to refuse medications, but it is *not* the student's right to behave disruptively. Therefore, if students have been allowed to remain on campus despite their disruptive behavior, I would recommend that they be advised in the following manner: "It is my impression that it is decidedly in your interest to resume your use of the medications since they seem to help you function better. Nonetheless, whether or not you use medications is really your business and your decision to make. However, I must warn you that, whether you use medications or not, your disruptive behavior on this campus will not be tolerated and its recurrence will result in the imposition of disciplinary sanctions." To eliminate any ambiguity that might ensue from this discussion, those sanctions should be spelled out immediately.

The above statement takes into account the reasonable possibility that certain students might resume their use of prescribed medications and yet continue to behave in a disruptive manner. After all, these medications, like psychotherapy itself, are not panaceas for disruptiveness. As one can easily imagine, the prevalent practice on many college campuses of insisting that the disruptive student use prescribed medications might lead many such students to assume, mistakenly and conveniently, that once they have resumed their use of medications they have fulfilled all behavioral obligations. They must be reminded, therefore, that the primary requirement is not their adjunctive use of medications but, rather, their reasonable conformity to the codes of student conduct.

One final caveat regarding the matter of medications: Quite often, a student's failure to use prescribed, stabilizing medications is experimental (to see how he or she might cope without them) and short-lived. If students' disruptive behavior appears to be a direct result of their failure to use medications and they have heretofore been generally conducting themselves nondisruptively on the campus, it might be well to regard these factors as extenuating circumstances that militate for a lesser sanction. Of course, a recurrence would probably bring a greater sanction.

THE DISRUPTIVE NON-STUDENT

It is quite common for many campuses, especially, it seems, those located near high schools, to encounter disruptive behavior that involves persons who are not enrolled at the college. At times, high school students, who may consider the staid atmosphere of the college to be an ideal target for their playful or malicious antics, will willfully vandalize or steal college property. And, to make matters worse, now and then a psychotic person will wander onto the campus from the community and create a public rumpus in the library or in the bookstore. What are the college's rights in this regard?

In California, a penal code (Section 626.6) gives the college the right to direct a non-student to leave the campus if that person is not otherwise required to be on campus and if it appears to the designated administrator that the non-student is committing an act likely to interfere with the peaceful conduct of the activities of the campus, or has come to the campus for that purpose.

Non-students, as required by the code, must follow such directions to leave, or they may be charged with a misdemeanor. Repeat visits within seven days are also misdemeanors. After seven days, directions to leave are dependent on the non-student once again appearing to commit an act likely to interfere with the peaceful conduct of college activities.

Section 626.6 does not on its face require any hearing. At the time a person is directed to leave, the person should be told what he or she has done to cause the direction and should also have an opportunity to respond orally before leaving. Documentation of the incident(s) and the college's response should be preserved. All states have similar trespass statutes that enable college authorities to bar dangerous and troublesome persons from the campus after a warning. College personnel should consult the trespass statutes in their own states in order to determine the extent of their particular jurisdiction in dealing with disruptive behavior involving non-students.

One administrator at a recent workshop asked about the college's rights in dealing with an enrolling student who had committed disruptive acts on the campus *before* he had officially enrolled. In such cases, the college cannot justifiably discipline a student for misconduct that was committed prior to the student's enrollment (assuming that the college had not already done so under a trespass statute). However, as I advised the administrator, it would be perfectly appropriate for him to meet with the incoming student and to advise him in the following manner:

- "Your conduct on this campus prior to your enrollment has been disruptive and objectionable in the following respects." (The administrator may then spell out those forms of behavior that were deemed disruptive).

- "If you had been a student at the time, you would have been in violation of the following codes of student conduct." (The administrator may then produce the codes of student conduct and specify which codes would have been violated had this person been a student at the time.)

- "Since your disruptive behavior seems to have followed a repetitive pattern, I thought it best to warn you that if you continued to behave disruptively, I would find it necessary, now that you are a student here, to recommend that certain disciplinary measures be imposed upon you." (The administrator may then specify those possible sanctions; loss of privileges, suspension, expulsion.)

CHILD CARE

I have received many reports from directors and supervisors of on-campus child care facilities regarding the (mis)conduct of students who are employed as child care workers. One concern that sometimes arises relates to the student's possible history of criminal conduct, especially as it may relate to the prior abuse of children or the psychiatric disorder known as paedophilia. Supervisors of these programs naturally want to know the extent of their legal rights to prohibit the employment of persons who have been convicted of child abuse.

Although it behooves a director of a college child care program to first consult a college administrator and/or an attorney before denying employment to an applicant because of a prior conviction for child abuse, in the end, barring employment to such individuals is probably legally permissible and warranted. After all, child abuse is a very serious crime and probably has resulted in the severe traumatization of one or more children.

In addition, the institution itself will probably be liable for any improper acts committed by such an employee which harm any children, and individual college employees may themselves be personally liable in damage suits if they were negligent in looking into the backgrounds of persons who would be working with vulnerable children. Therefore, the director may legitimately ask on an application form or in an interview whether the applicant has ever been convicted for the crime of child abuse. If the applicant answers in the affirmative, the director has, more than likely, sufficient grounds for denying employment to him or her. If the applicant answers in the negative and it is later somehow discovered that he or she has lied, this could be sufficient grounds for firing the student/employee.

Although the laws may vary from state to state, generally child abuse is a crime and any college employee who, during the course of carrying out his or her professional duties, learns of the abuse of any person under the age of eighteen is required by law to report that abuse to the proper authorities (either the police or the child protective service agency in the vicinity of the college). Thus, if a student, or for that matter, non-student, child care worker commits an act of child abuse within the college's child care facility, that act of abuse is obligatory grounds both for reporting the misconduct to an off-campus law enforcement or child protective service agency and to a college administrator.

The administrator, given the circumstances, should take immediate action by temporarily suspending the student from further work in the child care setting, at least until an administrative investigation either substantiates or invalidates the charges.

Incidentally, many acts of child abuse are difficult for directors precisely to define. For example, many child care workers fondle children with genuine and nonviolative affection. Others cross the line of acceptability by behaving in highly erotic, exhibitionistic or voyeuristic ways that clearly violate the physical and emotional rights of children.

In this regard, I was recently asked by a workshop participant what I thought of an incident that involved a female student/child care worker who was found masturbating in front of her charges (I later learned that this supervisor of a child care program was very dissatisfied with an administrator's decision to delay action on this case). I replied that this student's behavior was not only unacceptable, but that it constituted a form of child abuse that should have been reported. In any case, if directors of on-campus child care programs are not clear about how to define child abuse, or about their legal prerogatives to report such misconduct, they should consult an attorney and/or the child protective service agency in their locale.

A RESTROOM PROBLEM

From time to time, college officials express concerns, usually with an air of bemusement, about the occasional student whose entitlement to a gender-designated restroom has been questioned by other students. These cases usually involve students who are male tranvestites (a person who adopts the dress, manner and role of the opposite sex) who, meritedly or not, regard themselves as sufficiently of the female gender to be entitled to use the women's restroom. Because these students frequently have pronounced male characteristics—large bones, substantial height and facial hirsuteness—that belie their adopted feminine role, they are quickly detected and reported by female students, who, understandably, object to their use of the women's restroom.

When questioned, the student transvestite may claim, with complete sincerity and candor, that he no longer regards himself as a man and that he, therefore, has a rightful entitlement to use the women's restrooms of the campus. Furthermore, he is truly baffled by the indignant objections of his female soulmates who, in his view, should welcome him into their ranks by allowing him to share their restrooms. Is there a Solomonic solution to this problem that respects each person's rights and privileges without offending, embarrassing, or inconveniencing the contending principals?

One solution that was attempted by a college administrator was to arrange to have a separate restroom set aside on the campus for the convenience of the student transvestite. When this was proposed to him, however, he balked, stating that this arrangement was discriminatory and unacceptable in that it abrogated his legitimate right to use the women's restroom and, as a woman, he had the same legal rights as all other women students. It was at that juncture that I was consulted about this case.

In my view, a college that provides a student with a separate, private restroom of his own has already made unreasonable and unnecessary accommodations to that student. The student transvestite must realize that a college cannot be all things to all people. A college certainly should provide facilities and services that are both legally required and conducive to the well-being of the majority of its students. However, it cannot, and need not, transform itself into an institution that exquisitely meets the needs of all students. In short, there are no Solomonic or Utopian solutions to this particular problem. The rights to privacy of the objecting women students must be respected.

If a private restroom cannot be provided to the student transvestite, or if he objects to this arrangement, then he should be told that he is barred from using the women's restrooms and that, if he wishes he certainly may use the men's restrooms. (Of course, it remains to be seen whether the male students will eventually object to him on the grounds that his unorthodox appearance in the men's restrooms infringes on *their* rights of privacy).

Finally, if none of these options are available or acceptable to the student transvestite, he must be told to make his own arrangements for meeting nature's needs by leaving the campus and finding more hospitable facilities elsewhere. I may be mistaken, but I hardly think that such a student's demand to be allowed the use of women's restrooms on a college campus would be upheld in a court of law. As Steiner (1989, pg. 75) has pointed out, "The college does not owe a duty to a student that is higher than the duty owed by society at large."

COPING WITH EPITHETIC LANGUAGE OR SOCIALLY OFFENSIVE DRESS

In recent years colleges have certainly relaxed their standards regarding the language and dress of students. Anyone who spends any time moseying about the average college campus will hear many students and college employees alike use obscenities and vulgarisms with relative abandon. With some exceptions, such as at some religiously oriented or private schools, the language and dress of students are extended extremely wide latitude. Under the First Amendment, the right of free speech is vastly protected. But is that right absolute on the college campus?

Apparently not. Without undertaking an extensive review of court decisions on these matters, suffice it to say that students at public institutions of higher education enjoy rather unlimitedly free, constitutionally protected, political speech. However, public educational institutions can abridge a student's speech or dress in the following situations:

1. If the student's speech or dress demonstrably and adversely affects the health and safety of other members of the college community and;
2. If the student's speech demonstrably leads to a breach of the peace or seriously disrupts the educational processes of the college.

Recently, a college administrator sought advice regarding a student who had the epithet "Fuck You" emblazoned on his T-shirt. Evidently, this student's dress was not considered problematic until a female classmate registered a complaint, alleging that the epithet was a form of sexual harassment. The student who wore the epithetic T-shirt, when confronted with his classmate's allegation of sexual harassment and encouraged to relinquish the shirt, rejoined with the argument that it was his constitutional right to express himself in this manner. Fortunately, in recent years, women's legal protections against harassment from men have been broadened by prevailing law. The administrator, acutely aware of this fact, was at his wit's end trying to decide whose legal rights should prevail in this sticky case.

He was advised in the following manner: (1) To seek legal advice from his college attorney and (2) To spend more time with the two disputants on an informal basis, appealing to their sense of fair play and goodwill, and to the overriding need for compromise in such conflictual situations. Perhaps, too, friends or other persons who know and are trusted by the disputants could intercede and play a constructive role in mollifying them and resolving the crisis.

Sometimes, when college officials become overly anxious about a legal dispute between students and a prospective lawsuit against the college, they lose sight of the need to approach contentious students in a non-authoritative, non-blaming and even-tempered manner. Subtly, but significantly, contentious students often sense how much they may be unnerving an administrator with their complaints and, as result, they themselves become more anxious and intransigent. Often, indefatigable patience, humor, and a a good dose of lively imagination will enable the administrator to resolve and weather such crises far more than an immediate and dire invocation of the law.

Chapter VIII

Case Studies

The following cases involving disruptive students are not hypothetical. In Case 1, I served in the role of both principal complainant and consultant to a college administrator. In Case 2, my dual role was that of therapist for the complainants (who were students) as well as consultant to the college administration. In Cases 3 and 4, my principal role was that of consultant for the complainants (who were instructors). In Case 5, I provided consultation to both the complainant (an instructor) and the student who had been identified as disruptive.

These cases were selected because they seem to represent many of the typical disjunctions, misunderstandings, disagreements (philosophical and personal) and even bitter enmities that often arise when complainants and administrators fail—as so often happens—to see eye-to-eye on how to evaluate and resolve a disruptive crisis.

These cases are included primarily to illustrate the application of those principles outlined in the previous chapters, therefore my narrative will be interspersed with many references to those principles. Certain, largely inconsequential, facts have been altered and disguised in order to protect the privacy and confidentiality of the principals, with, obviously, the sole exception being my own identifiable role in each case. In all other respects I will attempt to provide a fair, balanced, and accurate depiction of the events as they occurred while fully appreciating the fact that my own vantage point may not completely encompass other, quite valid, perspectives and opinions regarding these cases.

I. You Can't Tell Me Where To Go!

Unlike most cases of disruptiveness on my campus, the following is a case of a student whose disruptive behavior caused me to intervene directly.

The odd saga of events began at a staff Christmas party at the student health center. The student, Ms. Lewis, a woman in her late twenties, entered the lunch room unannounced and (as I later learned) uninvited, and in the midst of the party, proceeded to garner a large plate of food from the table. Noticing that the staff was nonplused by her bold and unheralded visit, she casually mentioned that she had received permission to partake of the food by the chairperson of her department. Since the chairperson had never before extended such permission to students, and moreover, had not forewarned us about this student's planned foray, I was skeptical about the veracity of the excuse the student had given for her actions. The next time I saw the chairperson, I asked her if she had indeed given permission to the student to attend the Christmas party for the purpose of garnering some food. The chairperson emphatically denied even knowing that the student wished to attend the Christmas party. At the time, I considered it best to simply ignore the matter.

Not long after, one of our staff, a secretary, discovered Ms. Lewis mounted atop a tall ladder from which she was attempting to change a ceiling light bulb in the student health center. As the secretary, Ms. Harding, readily understood, repairs and other maintenance work of this kind were always assigned to the custodial staff of the department of buildings and grounds. A student who fell from a tall ladder and injured herself could very well hold the college legally responsible. Besides, Ms. Harding correctly thought, it was sheer chutzpah for the student to take it upon herself, without seeking permission from the staff to suddenly function in the role of college custodian. Thus, Ms. Harding firmly but politely asked the student to get down from the ladder immediately.

Following this incident, the student entered into a pattern of regularly coming into the clinic solely for the purpose of using its restrooms. Her behavior was a source of some inconvenience since it delayed or precluded the use of the restrooms by staff and by other students who were using the clinic's services for such purposes as urinanalysis. But, for a short time, the student's rather constant use of the restroom was ignored. That is, until Ms. Lewis began to use her regular sorties into the clinic further to annoy the secretarial staff.

One source of annoyance was the student's tendency to loiter in the clinic in order to rearrange the pamphlets and flyers that were lying about. On one occasion she told the secretary that she wanted to throw away the outdated pamphlets. Ms. Harding told her to leave them alone and that the staff would decide when to dispose of these materials.

Then the student switched tactics. In the waiting room was a candy dish that had been placed there by Ms. Harding with a card saying, "Take one, if you wish." On several occasions, Ms. Lewis was observed furtively snatching large handfuls of the candy, despite constant warnings from Ms. Harding not to do so. Again, no disciplinary measures were deemed necessary.

One day, in the early part of the fall semester, the clinic doors were locked shortly before closing time because only one nurse was on duty and several students were waiting to see her. Along came Ms. Lewis, and when she discovered that the door was locked, she began to shout angrily and unappeasedly at the secretarial staff to unlock it so she might use the restroom. Because her manner and language were considered highly abusive by the secretarial staff, they reported the incident to me the following day and requested that I do something about Ms. Lewis's chronic disruptiveness in the clinic.

At this juncture, I sent Ms. Lewis a note requesting that she come to my office for an interview. She came quite readily. I then transmitted to her in writing a request that she cease using the restrooms of the clinic unless she also used the clinic's services concurrently. I also pointed out in my written statement that her behavior in the clinic, going back to the Christmas party of the previous year, had been disruptive and that if such behavior continued, I would have to file a complaint against her with the college administration.

Point by point, I indicated which of her actions I considered disruptive and then alluded to those codes of student conduct that, in my estimation, she had violated. One was the code that prohibited the verbal abuse of staff, alluded to because of the shouting episode over the locked door. Another was the code that prohibited conduct that interfered with the normal operations of the college, which had applicability, in my view, because of her unauthorized attempt to change the ceiling light bulb and her rifling through the materials of the clinic with the intent to dispose of them.

After reading my statement, Ms. Lewis left the clinic in a huff, announcing as she left that she would take the matter up with the dean. I encouraged her to follow through on this plan since I too would be reporting the matter to the dean.

Soon thereafter, I spoke to the dean, requesting that he support our decision to bar Ms. Lewis from the clinic except during those times when she was utilizing its services. I then sent him a written report, documenting some of her prior disruptive behavior. When I next spoke with the dean I was surprised to learn that he had decided against intervening because the student told him she was required to use the clinic restrooms (which were located near her classes) because she had a certifiable disability—a bladder problem—which required, according to Ms. Lewis, frequent and immediate micturitions. She also stated to the dean that she was a counselee of the disabled student program because of this bladder problem. The dean informed me, with some indignation I thought, that he certainly could not discipline a student who suffered from such an unfortunate disability.

I told the dean that, given this student's demonstrated proclivity for lying, I thought it best that she be required to provide proof of this putative disability. My suspicion was that the student was most likely a counselee of the disabled student program but that the disability that qualified her to receive services in that program, considering her inordinately inappropriate behavior, was probably a psychiatric one.

Following my conversation with the dean, he called the disabled student program to ascertain whether Ms. Lewis was truly one of their counselees and, if so, the nature of her disability. He was told, quite correctly, that the status of any student in that program was completely confidential and could not be divulged without the student's written authorization. The dean then called me to say, with a good deal of irritation, that his efforts to help were being foiled by a lot of bureaucratic red tape. How could he possibly bar a student from the student health center who alleges that she has a physical disability that requires her to regularly use the clinic's restroom?

I replied that I thought it inappropriate for him to seek confirmation of the student's alleged disability from the staff of the disabled student program since they, obviously, could not give him this information without violating their policy of confidentiality. I suggested that the onus of providing proof of a disability was upon the student, Ms. Lewis, and therefore I recommended to the dean that he ask her to authorize release of information regarding her alleged medical disability from the disabled student program. He seemed reluctant to do this and for a brief period he and I had no more discussions about Ms. Lewis.

Ms. Lewis continued using the clinic restroom but added one rather clever and colorful variation to her behavior. Now she began to stop at Ms. Harding's desk each time she entered the clinic in order to request a Band-aid. The logic behind this behavior, evidently, was to fulfill our requirement that she receive some form of medical or psychological service in order to use the restroom. The Band-aids, in other words, were her passport into the clinic. Soon these constant requests for Band-aids became a rather disruptive and annoying sham. Therefore, I next advised the secretarial staff to refuse dispensing them unless the student agreed first to see a nurse, for, after all, anyone who was leaking that much blood several times a day should certainly receive medical attention.

After encountering our refusal to dispense Band-aids, Ms. Lewis again changed tactics. She made an appointment to see one of our nurses. She used this appointment to complain of a headache and then launched into a lengthy defense of her previous behavior in the clinic, while alleging that I must have something personal against her. The nurse, a relative newcomer to the staff, was unfamiliar with the various antecedents of the case and, therefore, only listened sympathetically to her litany of complaints.

Expecting that we were at the beginning of a new round of disruptive visits from Ms. Lewis, now under the guise of requiring medical help, I again contacted the dean, requesting his intervention. With considerable irritation, he told me that I was not doing my job and that I should take care of the problem. With equal annoyance, I told him I was indeed doing my job by responsibly reporting a seriously disruptive student in behalf of the entire clinic staff. I then went immediately to meet with him in his office.

As I correctly surmised, the dean, when he told me I was not doing my job, was already recognizing that Ms. Lewis was a person with a serious psychiatric disability and therefore he assumed, quite incorrectly in my view, that the best approach would be for me, a psychotherapist, to offer her psychotherapy as a remedy for her disruptiveness.

I told the dean that I was not going to offer Ms. Lewis therapy, that more than likely she had already received many hours of therapy elsewhere and that the problem of her disruptiveness should be dealt with on an administrative/disciplinary basis. I also told him that I did not appreciate being told that I was not doing my job when it was evident that I was definitely following acceptable guidelines in handling this matter. The dean feigned not remembering that he had accused me of not doing my job, but just in case he had, he apologized to me. After accepting his apology, I asked what he intended to do next.

He stated that he did not feel comfortable disciplining a student with a disability because that could lead to legal entanglements. I replied by telling him that, in my view, this student, whether or not she had a disability, clearly had no right to behave disruptively on the campus. I cited to him the legal principle that allows a college to discipline a student for misconduct, even when that misconduct is directly related to his/her physical or mental disability.

The dean remained unconvinced. I told him that I thought his fears of a lawsuit litigated by Ms. Lewis were largely groundless. But, I added with intense conviction, the staff of the Student Health Service and I were quite ready to file a lawsuit against the college if Ms. Lewis, who had already been reported many times as a highly disruptive student, should in any way cause us physical or emotional injury.

Following this discussion, the dean sent Ms. Lewis a certified letter to her home, informing her that she was not to enter the Student Health Center other than for the legitimate purpose of receiving medical and/or psychological services. This letter was essentially a kind of administrative restraining order. Ms. Lewis complied with the terms of this restraining order for a short time, but then she reverted to form by once again telling the dean that she was the victim of discrimination since her disability—now described as a serious allergy to tobacco smoke that was prevalent in the women's restrooms on the campus—required that she use the smoke-free restroom in the Student Health Center. The dean this time requested that Ms. Lewis adduce some proof of the alleged disabilities that required her to use the clinic restroom. Since she could not, the restraining order remained in effect.

The last time Ms. Lewis came to the clinic in order to use the restroom, she was accosted by Ms. Harding, who reminded her that she was under administrative order not to enter the premises unless it was for the purpose of receiving clinic services. She then quickly brandished a note supposedly written by a state disability agency that authorized her to have ready access to medical facilities in time of need. Ms. Harding told Ms. Lewis that she would have to discuss the matter with me.

When Ms. Lewis came into my office I asked if she might like to sit down. She refused. I then told her that I had heard she was in possession of a letter that permitted her to use the clinic. Might I see it? She showed me a letter that did boast at its top the letterhead of a disability agency. The letter was vaguely and almost illegibly written and said nothing about Ms. Lewis's special privileges to use any clinic, including the Student Health Center. I told Ms. Lewis that the letter did not enhance her privileges to use the clinic. Although she would always be welcome to use the clinic for medical or psychological services, the dean's restraining order would continue to be in effect and if she violated the terms of that order, I would report her to the dean and request that she be disciplined for misconduct. She again left in a huff, but this time she did not come back. She has since been seen many times passing the clinic, presumably on her way to restrooms elsewhere on the campus.

II. Let Me Show You My Etchings!

The early February morning began ordinarily enough, with a drizzly San Francisco fog. The first two students I saw that morning were indeed beset by serious personal crises but, fortunately, none of the irremediable kind.

While taking a short breather after the second session, I received a phone call from an instructor in the Science Building, informing me that a student who had been recently raped was in his office and in need of immediate attention. Putting aside my scheduled duties, I went directly to the instructor's office where I found a relatively young student (whom I shall call Ms. Dowd) sobbing uncontrollably.

Overcome by inconsolable dread and anguish, she informed me that only a few minutes before she had encountered on the campus the man who had raped her earlier that week. Ms. Dowd stated that the alleged rapist (whom I shall refer to as Mr. Mason), who was also a City College student, did not overtly threaten or mistreat her during their inadvertent encounter—he merely smiled and waved in her direction when they met—but, considering the fact that he had raped her only a few days before, she understandably perceived his mere presence to pose a definite menace to her safety.

Ms. Dowd revealed that she had already reported the rape to the Sex Crimes Unit of the San Francisco Police Department, which rapidly assisted her in receiving essential medical care. She asked if I would also assist her by contacting the sex crimes unit in order to ascertain the status of her case. I agreed to do this and then encouraged her to see me the following day for psychological counseling. She readily consented to this suggestion.

After determining that Ms. Dowd felt confident enough to go home unescorted, I returned to my office and placed a call to the sex crimes unit and was referred to Inspector Harper. Inspector Harper informed me that Ms. Dowd's charges were being duly investigated, however, I should understand that such complicated cases might take some time to resolve.

Before the end of our conversation, Inspector Harper asked me for a favor the nature of which left me momentarily flabbergasted. He stated that Ms. Dowd was evidently not the only City College student raped by Mr. Mason. He indicated that another woman (whom I shall call Ms. Miner) toward the end of the previous year had also reported having been raped by Mr. Mason. Inspector Harper said that he was having difficulty reaching Ms. Miner and, therefore, needed my help in finding her phone number through the college registrar's office. He then asked me to call her to say that he had been unsuccessfully attempting to reach her himself.

I called Ms. Miner, introduced myself, explained that I had just intervened in assisting a student rape victim and apprised her of Inspector Harper's wishes to speak with her. As tactfully as possible, I asked her if it was true that she too had been a recent victim of rape, taking strict precautions not to mention the name of the man accused of raping Ms. Dowd. Ms. Miner answered without hesitation that she had been raped almost two months before. Elaborating, she went on to say that she had immediately reported the crime to Inspector Harper, identifying the rapist as a fellow student named John Mason.

I then disclosed to Ms. Miner that Mr. Mason had been accused of raping another City College student and was consequently now under investigation for two separate crimes of rape, whereupon she assured me that she would certainly contact Inspector Harper in order further to pursue her own case. I asked Ms. Miner if she would care to see me for psychological counseling and she emphatically said she would soon arrange to do so.

The next day Ms. Dowd and I met in my office. Still in her late adolescence, Ms. Dowd could easily have been mistaken for a high school student. With little prompting, she provided a rather detailed account of her traumatic experiences of a few days before. She stated that she and Mr. Mason had known each other as acquaintances for a short time when they left the campus together to get something to eat at a local fast-food restaurant. Mr. Mason suggested that they take the food to his apartment where they could chat, relax, and he could show her the place. Actually, as later came to light, this apartment belonged to a friend and was expediently borrowed for the purpose of enticing and raping Ms. Dowd.

Once in the apartment, Mr. Mason feigned an interest in showing Ms. Dowd the furnishings and arrangements of the rooms until they eventually found themselves in the bedroom. Suddenly his charm and hospitality vanished, replaced by a cold, stern command that she submit to his sexual desires. Ms. Dowd, astonished and dismayed by such a radical and ominous turnabout in Mr. Mason's manner, repeatedly and obstinately protested, thereby clearly declaring her nonconsent. Finding it impossible to break her will by means of sheer verbal insistence, Mr. Mason resorted to a direct threat, stating that he would physically harm Ms. Dowd if she continued to remonstrate with him. Out of fear for her physical well-being, if not her very life, she remorsefully succumbed.

I found Ms. Dowd's account of her experience entirely convincing and credible. She evinced such absolute horror and anguish over her terrifying recollections that even a veteran therapist such as myself, who has heard the painful narratives of literally thousands of student clients, including scores of rape victims, could not help but be deeply moved by the ordeal she had been through.

At the end of our first session, Ms. Dowd and I formulated a plan to continue the therapy for an indefinite period. I also informed her that I would, with her permission, report this matter to an appropriate college administrator who could perhaps initiate an administrative investigation into the charges. She granted me permission to transmit this report and soon thereafter I received a reply from the dean, who requested that I arrange to have Ms. Dowd come in person to his office to file charges against Mr. Mason.

A few days later I met with Ms. Miner. A slight, attractive woman in her early twenties, Ms. Miner portrayed her victimization in a manner remarkably similar to Ms. Dowd's. Ms. Miner and Mr. Mason had briefly and casually known each other at City College when he invited her to have dinner with him a local restaurant. After dinner, he invited her to "his" apartment.

After a sham tour of the rooms, he cornered her in the bedroom and declared his sexual intentions. Ms. Miner evidently was a bit more resistive than Ms. Dowd because Mr. Mason found it necessary to slap her several times to demonstrate that he meant business before she yielded to his wishes. As was the case with Ms. Dowd, I found nothing suspect or incredible about Ms. Miner's rendition of her rape experience. She also agreed to allow me to request an administrative investigation of her charges.

The following week, Ms. Dowd and I met for our second session. Just moments after the session ended I received a call on the intercom from the clinic's secretary requesting that I come out to the waiting room immediately. In the waiting room I found Ms. Dowd crying and gesticulating frantically. In a rapid barrage of words she explained that when she had returned to the waiting room her grandmother, who had escorted her to the campus without knowing that her granddaughter had been a victim of rape, was pointing to a man who had been continuously and suspiciously staring into the clinic a few feet from its entrance. When Ms. Dowd looked out, she was horrified to see Mr. Mason peering in. Evidently, when he saw the bustle he was causing inside the clinic, he took off, since my prompt inspection of the area surrounding the clinic uncovered no clues as to his whereabouts.

After arranging for the campus police to escort Ms. Dowd and her grandmother from the college, I placed a call to the then president of the college, informing him that we had, in my estimation, two cases of rape coupled with harassment that warranted speedy administrative intervention. He promised that he would personally look into the matter and advised me to consult with the dean to whom the matter had been originally reported.

The dean and I met and he expressed concern that neither alleged rape victim had as yet scheduled a conference or submitted a formal complaint with him, despite my encouragement that they do so immediately. This was definitely hamstringing his efforts to intervene. Apparently, unbeknownst to me, both Ms. Dowd and Ms. Miner had been reticent and procrastinative about initiating an investigation through the college's administrative channels because, according to what they later told me, they had little faith that the college would adequately defend or protect their interests. I later assured them that, their misgivings notwithstanding, it was definitely in their best interest to file a report with the dean.

When I next spoke with the dean he and I resolved to meet with Mr. Mason in order to question him regarding the allegations of the two alleged rape victims. Strictly following the advice of Inspector Harper, we did not in this meeting directly confront him with his accusers since that would likely have undermined the process of identification that was to be undertaken at a later time by the judicial system. Inspector Harper cautioned me not to do anything that would appear to tamper with the judicial investigation, since such actions could ultimately destroy all grounds for the arrest and conviction of Mr. Mason.

Mr. Mason surprised me. I somehow expected to meet a much larger and more formidable man. Small, thin and wiry, his physical appearance clashed with the image I had been harboring of a towering figure who could easily overpower any woman. Of course, I had things confused. It was easy to see why his victims could trust and be tricked by him. His physical diminutiveness and polite, almost chivalric, speech could certainly be considered prepossessing. At second glance, however, it was also easy to see that he was physically strong, certainly far more powerful than either of the two women who independently identified him as her rapist.

Mr. Mason not only denied committing acts of rape but imperturbably stated that he had never met or heard of the two women who had accused him of raping them. He then went on to say that he could not have committed such heinous crimes since he was himself the father of a daughter and, furthermore, an upstanding Christian.

It was not only Mr. Mason's blatant non sequiturs that aroused my suspicions. First, it seemed totally implausible that two women could independently and cogently identify him as their rapist without his even knowing either of them. Even more telling, in my view, however, was Mr. Mason's manner throughout our interview. I thought it quite fascinating that he seemed so devoid of either indignation or distress in the face of such serious charges. On the contrary, his imperturbability, marked by an almost graceful matter-of-factness, had an eerie quality. It seemed to me that a truly innocent person would have suffered a great deal more perturbation over multiple allegations of committing rape.

At the end of our meeting I conferred briefly with the dean. I informed him that, although I couldn't of course prove it, I definitely thought Mr. Mason had been lying to us when he denied either knowing or raping the two women. I reminded the dean of the fact that Mr. Mason was seen stalking one of the two complainants, Ms. Dowd, at the Student Health Center. I, therefore, recommended that the college take whatever measures were legally allowable to protect not only the two complainants, but any other unsuspecting college women who might be victimized by him in the future.

After all, I averred, even if he had not yet been convicted of a crime, he was a prime suspect in two rape cases involving City College students and therefore his actions on the campus should be placed under some form of control and surveillance. Perhaps, I also opined, if he is eventually arrested for the rape of the two City College students he should also be temporarily suspended until his case was fully adjudicated in the courts. (Apropos of the opinion I had expressed to the dean, the reader might find it interesting and useful to learn that Towson State University in Maryland has recently instituted a policy to suspend, automatically, students accused of rape if administrators ascertain from police there is reason to believe an assault has actually occurred.)

In response to this request, the dean sent Mr. Mason written notification that, in case he really did know these women, he was administratively enjoined from having any contact with them on the college campus.

A few days later I met for the second time with Ms. Miner. She brought with her an address book. On a page toward the middle of the book were the handwritten name and telephone number of Mr. Mason. Ms. Miner stated that Mr. Mason himself had written his name and phone number in her address book after she had requested him to do so while on their date. I made a copy of this page and later compared the signature of Mr. Mason in Ms. Miner's address book with his signature on the medical form in his student health service file.

Although I am by no means a graphologist, even my inexpert eye easily discerned the remarkable similarities between the two signatures. If there had been any doubt in my mind that Mr. Mason had known Ms. Miner, this new evidence entirely dispelled it. I reported this newfound evidence to Inspector Harper, who advised me to retain it because it would probably be useful in later judicial proceedings.

My next step was to meet with the president of the college to advocate aggressive administrative action in behalf of the two rape victims. I advocated that, now that there seemed to be sufficient evidence to indicate that Mr. Mason had known the two complainants, perhaps a more formal and extensive hearing could flush out the entire truth. In reply, the president explained that because Mr. Mason had not yet even been arrested for rape and administrative interventions could not precede or supersede the judicial process in such matters, there was nothing more the college could do to protect the alleged victims.

Furthermore, he added, the alleged crimes took place in the off-campus San Francisco community, well beyond the administrative jurisdiction of the college. In reply, I stated that it seemed unfortunate that the college, unlike some other colleges, did not include in its code of student conduct some provision for dealing with cases in which it could be established that a student's off-campus conduct adversely affected the interests of the college. Also, I added, Mr. Mason's on-campus stalking behavior toward Ms. Dowd certainly could be disciplined without awaiting decisions that emanated from off-campus judicial proceedings.

The president then suggested that I was advocating a course of action that could result in a lawsuit against the college, litigated, of course, by Mr. Mason. Quite correctly, in my view, he suggested that if the college in any way tampered with or disrupted Mr. Mason's education by instituting disciplinary procedures against him, and he eventually was proven innocent of the charges, he might successfully sue the college. The president had already consulted the college's attorneys on this matter and this was their authoritative opinion.

In response, I argued that, despite my lack of legal expertise, I confidently believed that the college was on the horns of a legal dilemma. I pointed out that if either of the two alleged rape victims was revictimized by Mr. Mason as a result of the school's failure to fully investigate the charges against him and to place proportionate administrative constraints upon his actions on campus, *she* could successfully sue the school. And, further to complicate matters, I stated, if Mr. Mason were to victimize any other City College students *after* the time at which we had already become aware of the allegations against him and had done too little to investigate or monitor his on-campus behavior, *those students* could successfully sue the college.

My legal arguments did not possess the powers of suasion. The president suggested that it may have been a serious mistake on my part to have held the investigative meeting with Mr. Mason since even that procedure could be considered an actionable abuse of college authority. I strongly disagreed, stating that the dean and I, in that meeting, did not level either criminal charges or accusations against Mr. Mason, but merely questioned him regarding his knowledge of the alleged rapes. We were, I was convinced, only exercising our legitimate institutional prerogatives.

My meeting with the president ended in an uneasy stalemate, neither of us bending very far from his original position. Before leaving the meeting, I mentioned to the president that if and when Mr. Mason was arrested I would possibly ask the college newspaper to cover the story. I said that I wanted to alert all City College women to the fact that he was a prime suspect in the rape of two of our students. My rationale for disseminating this information was to encourage women students to be especially circumspect and vigilant in their dealings with this man. After all, few women, in my estimation, would be eager to associate with, let alone date, a man who had just been arrested for multiple crimes of rape. A college newspaper story about the arrest might serve as a deterrent and save other women from a great deal of grief.

The president's wince at the mention of possible newspaper coverage of the case clearly bespoke his aversion for such publicity. He stated that, although he thought such publicity ill-advised, he would respect my right to do as I saw fit.

Over the next several months I maintained regular contact with Inspector Harper and with the office of the San Francisco District Attorney (to which I offered to serve, if necessary, as a witness in the case) in order precisely to assess and monitor the progress of the investigation. I also continued to have periodic individual therapy sessions with the two rape victims (who, incidentally, had never met and did not know each other's identity) in order to offer them optimal emotional support throughout the proceedings as well as to assist them in deciphering and dealing with the myriad complexities of the judicial system.

The process of positively identifying Mr. Mason as the actual perpetrator of the rapes was a frustratingly protracted one, unduly delayed by several unexpected factors. First, the friend whose apartment Mr. Mason borrowed to commit the crimes of rape was also named John. This coincidence naturally caused the District Attorney's office to be especially painstaking and heedful in its investigation since there existed a risk, albeit remote, that the wrong John might be identified as the culprit. Second, there had been considerable delay in the transmission of a photograph of Mr. Mason from the Department of Motor Vehicles to Inspector Harper with which the rape victims might positively identify him.

Finally, on the day Ms. Miner was being brought in by the police to identify Mr. Mason, she, in a moment of panic, instead mistakenly identified to the officers an innocent passerby on the campus as her rapist. At the exact time of this false identification Mr. Mason was firmly ensconced in one of the offices of the police department where he was being detained for questioning.

This case of mistaken identification, caused no doubt by a long and miserable accumulation of dread and anxiety, totally disqualified Ms. Miner as a reliable witness in this case, according to Inspector Harper. Without being very conversant with the judicial requirements for rape victims to serve as qualified witnesses in their own behalf, it seemed to me eminently unfair to disqualify Ms. Miner as a reliable witness because she once and only momentarily identified someone else as her rapist on the very same day that she was being brought in for questioning; on a day, in other words, when she most certainly felt overwrought and confused. Although I did not verbally gainsay the decision of the police, I thought they had compounded Ms. Miner's mistake with a far more egregious and tragic one when they disqualified her as a witness.

Judicial obstacles and delays notwithstanding, Mr. Mason was eventually arrested for the rape of Ms. Dowd. He was quickly released on $25,000 bail and, according to Ms. Dowd, who had seen him on the campus the next day, was evidently once again attending City College classes with impunity. Troubled over this news, I went to the campus newspaper, requesting that it report Mr. Mason's arrest in its next edition. An article under the headline, "CCSF Student Charged in Alleged Rape Case," appeared soon thereafter. I was correctly quoted in the article as saying, "Students should be alerted to the possibility that this man is on campus, and to the fact that he has been arrested on suspicion of being a rapist. They should be aware of this fact so they can make their own informed decision about how much to associate with such an individual."

Soon after the article appeared, I was summoned to the president's office to discuss what he deemed to be the adverse nature of this publicity. There were strong undertones of vexation in the president's manner and speech when he clearly implied that I had seriously transgressed by enlisting the help of the campus newspaper to create a public drumbeat about a case of an alleged student rapist. I am sure it was just not my imagination that caused me to think that I was being accused by the president of unjustly convicting and pillorying a man who had not yet been judicially tried, let alone convicted, for any crime whatsoever.

My tete-a-tete with the president became a bit heated; two decent men, I thought, trying their utmost to balance the constitutional rights of one accused man with the legal rights of thousands of City College women to receive the highest possible degree of physical protection and safety from their college. Although I was clearly the more cantankerous of the two, I believe I was entirely correct when I insisted that at no point throughout the investigation had I in the slightest way violated Mr. Mason's academic or constitutional rights. And, I told the president, in my view, the college was morally derelict for not taking a more aggressive posture in protecting its women students in this case.

Toward the end of the meeting, the president indicated, almost as an aside, that he had received some irksome phone queries from members of the college board of governors about the newspaper article. I assumed that it was those calls that bestirred the president to chide me, as he had never done before, about my professional conduct.

Late in the year, just a few days before he was to appear in court, and almost an entire year after the first victim, Ms. Miner, filed criminal charges against him, Mr. Mason plea bargained. He pled guilty to a charge of felony assault. He was sentenced to spend a year in the county jail and placed on probation for three years. In assessing the outcome of this case, the district attorney was quoted as saying, "There was a 95 percent chance that if Mr. Mason had been convicted of rape, he would have gotten the minimum sentence due to the fact that it was his first offense, it wasn't violent, and other reasons. He probably would have gotten out in a year-and-a-half anyway. So, we are pleased with the outcome. It gives us some control over him as opposed to trying him for rape, losing, and the guy walks out."

I do not know if Mr. Mason has ever attempted to re-enroll at City College (this case took place about five years ago). I suspect not. I also suspect that the college would now have sufficient grounds for prohibiting his enrollment, if it wished; not necessarily because he committed a vicious off-campus crime against two City College students, but, ironically, because while on the campus, in a formal investigative hearing, he deliberately and glaringly lied to college officials about the extent of his acquaintance with the two students who charged him with his crimes. Those lies clearly obstructed the judicial processes of the college and therefore punishably violated the college code of student conduct.

III. Me and My Shadow ...

Ms. Clarke was assigned to be Ms. Todd's academic advisor. Ms. Todd was a first-year student who requested help with selecting her courses and generally navigating her way through some of the complications and snags in the institutional system. Ms. Todd, as she initially appeared to Ms. Clarke, was a wispy, childlike person who, despite a kind of insatiable neediness, was not in the least threatening.

After meeting somewhat irregularly for several months in order to discuss her academic concerns, Ms. Todd one day unexpectedly announced to Ms. Clarke that she had a crush on another person. She was rather cryptic and reticent in discussing this matter, so Ms. Clarke did not pursue it further. When Ms. Todd once again brought up the subject of her deep affection for this other individual, she asked Ms. Clarke's advice about how to handle her feelings. Specifically, she wanted to know if she should divulge her feelings to this new heartthrob. Ms. Clarke, assuming that these were the natural, innocent feelings of a nubile young woman, enthusiastically told Ms. Todd, "Go for it."

This type of exchange went on for several more months. Ms. Todd would ask Ms. Clarke what she thought of her feelings for her beloved, and Ms. Clarke would reply by encouraging her to express those feelings as openly as possible. Toward the end of the semester, Ms. Todd told Ms. Clarke that she had written some love poems to her sweetheart and wanted to know if she should actually send them to that person. Ms. Clarke, once again assuming that Ms. Todd was simply playing the innocent role of the coquettish ingenue, encouraged her to share her poetry with her newfound turtledove. Ms. Todd left and when she returned she brought back her love poems and gave them to Ms. Clarke. It was only then that Ms. Clarke, dumbstruck by this unexpected turn of events, discovered that she was the true recipient of Ms. Todd's love overtures.

Without rancor or judgmental displeasure, but with unmistakable resolve, Ms. Clarke informed Ms. Todd that she could not reciprocate her feelings. She pointed out to her that, as her advisor, she was strictly interested in helping her with her academic pursuits. She made it immediately and perfectly clear that she did not want a personal or romantic relationship with Ms. Todd. Ms. Todd, obviously feeling rebuffed by this response, countered by saying that perhaps the problem could be solved by her dropping out of school. Then there would be no professional complications to interfere with their having a personal relationship. Ms. Clarke, steadfast in her wish to maintain a strictly professional relationship with Ms. Todd, told her that it would not matter if Ms. Todd left the college. She would not, in any case, wish to pursue the relationship on a personal basis.

Soon after this exchange took place, Ms. Clarke received a note from Ms. Todd. It contained some rather strong allusions to suicidal intentions. Alarmed by the content of this note, Ms. Clarke referred the matter to the college administration, requesting that they assist by investigating the matter.

At about this time, Ms. Todd also gave Ms. Clarke a large cash gift. The gift was immediately returned to her. Soon after being notified about this problem, the dean informed Ms. Todd that she was administratively barred from having further contact with Ms. Clarke. In one of her contacts with Ms. Clarke, Ms. Todd had informed her that she had been psychiatrically diagnosed as a schizophrenic and on at least one occasion was involuntarily hospitalized for perpetrating violence upon a family member.

Ms. Clarke was unclear about whether this information was confidential, but, considering its problematic nature, and after discussing the matter with an attorney, she decided to transmit the information to the dean, while requesting that he strictly maintain its confidentiality. To Ms. Clarke's dismay, the dean sent copies of her report to several other persons at the college, including, for some inexplicable reason, Ms. Todd herself. Understandably irked by the dean's disclosures, Ms. Clarke expressed concern to him about the fact that he may have, by forwarding her report to Ms. Todd, placed her in a legally vulnerable position.

Following these incidents, Ms. Todd began to stalk Ms. Clarke, off and on the campus. As Ms. Clarke traversed the campus during the course of her workday, she espied Ms. Todd hiding in the bushes and in various niches of hallways and the dining room, from which she would peer at her every movement. Then she began to receive mysterious phone calls at her home, placed, she confidently believed, by Ms. Todd. For a short time, Ms. Clarke had a friend who occasionally visited with her. One day she received a phone call from someone who asked to speak to that friend. Since no one had ever before made such a phone call to her house, she was naturally skeptical about the caller. After making a few inquiries about the caller, she recognized the voice—Ms. Todd's. The caller hung up before she could be questioned further.

The dean, after reviewing Ms. Clarke's complaints, informed her that her reports, "Leave me cold." He told her that the student's rights to an education were paramount in this matter. He implied that the student could file a lawsuit should the college tamper with those rights. Ms. Clarke informed the dean that the student's rights did not abrogate or supersede her right to work in a safe academic environment, and that she expected the administration to take effective steps to protect her from harm at the hands of Ms. Todd.

The dean, apparently unaware of the proper grounds for disciplining students, told Ms. Clarke that, because Ms. Todd was a diagnosed schizophrenic, he could not "kick her out" on the basis of her mental illness. Ms. Clarke, not yet being familiar with the fact that Ms. Todd (or any other student) could certainly be disciplined for her *disruptive behavior*, whether or not she had a diagnosable mental illness, did not further argue the point with the dean.

Instead, she attempted to redress her grievances by consulting one of the vice-presidents, the dean's administrative subordinate. In the end, she felt that he, too, did not take her concerns seriously. She then consulted me. After receiving from her a quite detailed account of this evolving crisis, I suggested that we meet with the vice-president so that, together, we could perhaps state the case more convincingly. It was certainly my opinion, based upon Ms. Todd's ungovernable and potentially dangerous stalking of Ms. Clarke, that the college should take affirmative steps immediately to remove the student from the campus via a suspension or by some other means, at least until a formal hearing could be held. I told Ms. Clarke that I would repeat that recommendation in our meeting with the vice-president.

The meeting with the vice-president did not go as smoothly as I had hoped and expected. For reasons that only became clear much later, he was reluctant to use disciplinary procedures to deal with Ms. Todd. I shared my observation that the student had already seriously violated the student code of conduct by repeatedly behaving in an invasive and disruptive manner toward Ms. Clarke.

The vice-president indicated that he was not yet ready to impose discipline because Ms. Todd's behavior, however annoying it might be, was not so serious as to warrant disciplinary measures. It was difficult to fathom the vice-president's reasons for believing that a student who persistently menaced an instructor and was known to have been hospitalized for perpetrating violence upon a family member was not already considered to be dangerous enough to warrant at least a temporary suspension from the campus.

During the course of our meeting the vice-president indicated that he wanted my assistance in resolving the crisis. When I asked how, he stated that he wanted to send the student, Ms. Todd, to me in order to have her psychologically tested and evaluated. He suggested that this approach might enable him to take a more precise measure of her condition and, even more specifically, her potential lethality.

I told the vice-president that it would be entirely inappropriate for me or any other mental health professional to test and evaluate Ms. Todd in order to provide the college with grounds for dealing effectively with her. I supported my opinion with the following explanation:

1. Whether Ms. Todd eventually consented to such a procedure or not, it was at best a heavy-handed, coercive, and even somewhat devious measure that could create its own legal problems;
2. Any psychological data or findings that were generated by a psychological interview were largely confidential (unless, for example, the student revealed in the interview that she intended to kill herself or someone else), therefore, I would not be permitted, without the written authorization of the student, to share my findings with the vice-president anyway;
3. Predictions about the lethality of people, even when based upon intensive examinations by psychological experts, were not highly reliable, and, most importantly;
4. The college, by undertaking a psychological approach to this problem, would entirely miss the point. No one, including Ms. Clarke, objected to Ms. Todd because of her alleged mental illness.

She was deemed objectionable because her behavior was unruly, invasive, menacing, and grossly disrespectful of the rights of a college employee. Therefore, the college, in my view, should not attempt to enlist largely specious psychological findings in order to deal with a problem that essentially required a disciplinary approach.

Then, in a moment of lighthearted collegiality, I used, in my view, very bad judgment, by offhandedly remarking that, based upon the reports I had received about Ms. Todd, I would assume that the diagnosis of schizophrenia was correct. I made it clear, however, that my diagnostic impression was, of course, a secondhanded guess, and, because of its irrelevance, was to be considered entirely off-the-record.

The vice-president seemed uncomfortable with my recommendations but said he would take them under consideration. Following the meeting, Ms. Clarke asked me for a favor. She asked if I would document the conversation we had just had with the vice-president and send her a copy of my write-up. I consented to do this and later forwarded a copy to the vice-president. A few days later I received a very angry, vituperative letter from the vice-president (with carbon copies sent to several other college officials, including the then president), accusing me of "taking sides with the faculty" and of being "anti-administration." In the letter the vice-president expressed anger over the fact that I refused to use psychological interventions to resolve a campus crisis yet was quite willing to use a psychological diagnosis to describe a disruptive student's personality.

I considered the conflict with the vice-president to be very unfortunate because I had always liked and respected him a great deal (and still do), and I think, up to this point, he had reciprocated my feelings. Nevertheless, I firmly believed that he had unjustly accused me of being "pro-faculty" or "anti-administration" since for many years I had worked cooperatively with the college administration and even defended it against various faculty complaints even when I strongly disagreed with certain administrative practices. I therefore wrote him an angry letter of my own in which I recapitulated our discussion at the meeting and informed him that there were no genuine contradictions between my stated, official position regarding the handling of the case and my "off-the-record" speculation about Ms. Todd's mental status. (I was here paying for my mistake in verbalizing that speculation to the vice-president). To set the record straight, I sent carbon copies of my letter to the same college officials who had received the vice-president's letter. Finally, I requested a meeting with the Vice-President in order to iron out our differences.

We met a couple of days later. The meeting was fairly amicable. The vice-president revealed why he was so upset. It evidently had two causes. First, he did not expect me to document the proceedings of our meeting and therefore felt betrayed by my actions. I responded to this complaint by apologizing, while explaining that I, too, did not expect to document the proceedings but was later asked to do so by Ms. Clarke, and, considering it a very good idea myself, I consented to her request. I again apologized for not forewarning him about my ultimate decision to document the meeting.

The second cause of the vice-president's perturbation was more crucial and complicated. He stated that my documentation made it clear and very official that he and I held sharply antithetical and conflicting opinions about how the case should be resolved—his favoring non-disciplinary means and mine championing a strong, disciplinary approach. These differences of opinion could lead to serious trouble. He then went on to say that, should this case eventually find its way into a court of law, he and I would be on opposite sides. He believed that this placed him at a decided disadvantage since I was a well respected expert in my field and therefore could more capably convince a judge or a jury of the correctness of my position, or, conversely, the incorrectness of his. This possibility, he said, troubled him considerably.

I told the vice-president that I hoped he would understand that my position was not, as he had stated in his letter to me, inherently anti-administration. However, I did strongly oppose his position and had explicitly said so in our meeting with Ms. Clarke. Therefore, if this case, for whatever reason, did eventuate in a lawsuit, he could be quite sure that we would indeed be on opposite sides. I myself was not convinced, however, as was he, that my word in a court of law would be accorded any more respect than his.

In any case, as far as I could tell, our differences of opinion were no one's fault. It was often the nature of cases involving disruptive students that different college officials favored quite disparate courses of action. I was acting entirely out of professional integrity and, in my view, in the best interest of the college when I opposed his position. I hoped he would understand that rather than ascribe antagonistic motives to my actions.

As far as I could tell, the vice-president and I had forged a genuine rapprochement by the end of this meeting and we parted on very friendly terms. Still, something in his manner made me think that he was somehow more distressed with himself than with me.

Getting back to the case itself, Ms. Clarke, feeling stymied by the lack of administrative intervention, decided to take the matter to the president of the college. The gravity of Ms. Todd's disruptive behavior was pointed out to the president who, to Ms. Clarke's pleasant surprise, was sympathetic to her concerns.

He called for a formal hearing. A hearing was scheduled, to which Ms. Clarke was invited to appear as principal witness. Fearing for her safety, she at first refused to appear. She was then informed by the administrative staff that her refusal to appear would obstruct the judicial process, so she finally agreed to testify at the hearing. At the hearing, according to Ms. Clarke, Ms. Todd behaved in such a bizarre, deranged manner that it left no doubt in anyone's mind that this student posed a definite and imminent threat to the safety of others, especially Ms. Clarke.

Before a final disciplinary decision was made by the judicial officer, I received a phone call from Ms. Todd's private psychotherapist (who knew I had been serving as a consultant on the case) who reported to me, under the requirements of *Tarasoff* (the law that holds psychotherapists liable for failing to take reasonable care to warn a readily identifiable victim whom their client has threatened to harm), that Ms. Todd disclosed in her therapy an intention to harm Ms. Clarke. I immediately reported this information to Ms. Clarke who, if memory serves me correctly, had already been apprised of this threat. I then reported the threat to the vice-president, who indicated that he would have the college immediately seek a restraining order against Ms. Todd. For reasons that never became entirely clear to me, a restraining order was never issued.

After a short but frightening period of delay, the college finally imposed disciplinary sanctions upon Ms. Todd—a three-year suspension. To my knowledge, Ms. Todd's harassment of Ms. Clarke ceased at that point.

Over the last several years I have had several very friendly conversations with the vice-president, who now is an administrator at another college. Without sharing very many details about his role in this case, he has made it eminently clear, as I had earlier surmised, that he himself did not want to take a non-disciplinary approach toward Ms. Todd. However, because he was under strict instructions from the college attorney to, at all costs, avoid a lawsuit by assuming a "hands-off" administrative posture toward this student, he could not act otherwise. In short, he explained, he was basically in agreement with me at the time but was under duress to follow legal advice that was, in my estimation, dreadfully wrongheaded and, worse, dangerous.

IV. Disruptive, Disruptive ... *Who's* Disruptive?

An instructor sought my help with a case involving a student who was behaving disruptively in her department. She reported that this student, Robert Smith, a nineteen-year-old English major, had exhibited a pattern of creating havoc throughout the department and now one particularly distraught instructor wanted him thrown out of her class. In our conference she described him as a loudmouthed bully who refused to accept or respect the conventional rules of the classroom or the authority of his instructors. Specifically, he rudely and repeatedly interrupted lectures with irrelevant and belligerent comments, sought to embarrass his instructors by publicly suggesting that they were woefully unqualified to teach, and generally evinced a total disregard for the academic rights of his classmates.

I asked the instructor why she had come at this time. She stated that one of her colleagues was now totally fed up with Mr. Smith and if something were not done about him soon, she might quit her teaching position. This would be extremely unfortunate, she added, since the instructor, Ms. Morse, was a highly respected teacher of long-standing at the college. My informant asked me to speak with the chairperson of the department in order to elicit more information about Mr. Smith and to give him some advice about how to cope with the student's disruptiveness.

The chairperson corroborated the earlier report about Mr. Smith's history of disruptiveness in the department and then stated that he felt someone needed to take immediate action in order to avert a crisis since Ms. Morse, who had recently had a frightening confrontation with Mr. Smith over his disruptive behavior, was afraid to return to teach that class and was threatening to quit her job. He asked my advice.

I informed him that he and all other persons in the department, including Ms. Morse, should write individual reports that documented the nature of Mr. Smith's disruptive behavior. These reports should be written individually and include references to those specific forms of behavior that were deemed disruptive. The write-ups should include no speculation, psychological or otherwise, regarding the causes of Mr. Smith's behavior. The dates and sequence of events should be chronicled as accurately as possible. The report should be dated and, if the department or the instructor had a preference regarding how this problem should be resolved, that preference should be explicitly stated in the report. The reports should immediately be transmitted to the dean, with a request that he consult with the complainants as soon as possible.

The chairperson then asked for advice about how to defuse the situation immediately, since it seemed potentially dangerous and it might take many hours or days before the dean could formally intervene. I suggested that the chairperson advise Ms. Morse of her right to remove the student from her class for two consecutive sessions. By enforcing this right she could perhaps buy sufficient time to have the matter resolved at the administrative level. Ms. Morse followed through on this suggestion and the student was officially notified by the chairperson of his removal from two consecutive classes.

Despite this injunction, the student displayed a fierce determination to remain in the class. Therefore, on the day of the next class, an administrator notified the campus police of Mr. Smith's intention to enter Ms. Morse's class unlawfully, and just moments before the class was to convene, a large contingent of police officers cordoned off the area, blocking Mr. Smith's path as he attempted to enter the class. When I learned of this incident, I advised the chairperson to document it, since Mr. Smith's attempt to flout the injunction constituted, I thought, a rather flagrant violation of the code of student conduct. The chairperson did document the incident and transmitted his report to the dean.

When I first learned that Mr. Smith was identified as a disruptive student, I consulted a file that was kept in the Student Health Center containing the names of all students who had been previously reported as disruptive. Not surprisingly, Mr. Smith's name appeared in the file. About two years before he had been reported to me as disruptive by a sociology instructor.

Since I could not recall the details of her complaint, I called her. (I should explain at this juncture that since the students whose names were placed in that exclusive file were reported to the Mental Health Program as disruptive persons and were not in the file because they had been clients of the program, neither their names nor the incidents in which they were involved were confidential. If, by coincidence, they also at one time had been clients of the Mental Health Program, any information connected with their psychotherapeutic use of the program was kept strictly confidential.)

The sociology instructor, Ms. Barr, reminded me of the reasons she had filed a complaint against Mr. Smith two years before. Mr. Smith had badgered her, challenged her authority to teach, and generally conducted himself in an obnoxious and belligerent manner in her class. In short, his behavior was practically identical to the behavior that one of his current instructors, Ms. Morse, had reported. Ms. Barr put up with his behavior until he one day verbally abused her in the hallway by calling her a "bitch" and telling her he would "get" her. There were witnesses to this incident.

Pursuant to my advice at the time, she reported the series of incidents to the dean, who had the matter duly investigated. Unbeknownst to me, that investigation ended in a strange and, in my estimation, highly unsatisfactory denouement. Rather than discipline Mr. Smith for his offensive and overtly threatening behavior, the administrators who conducted the investigation simply reassigned him to another sociology instructor's class, attributing his behavior toward Ms. Barr to an unfortunate clash of personalities. Soon thereafter, when Ms. Barr raised questions about the wisdom of this decision—did it not extend carte blanche to Mr. Smith to continue behaving disruptively?—she was told by the administrators that it was too late to carry out any form of disciplinary action. This, in my view, compounded a serious mistake with a gratuitous lie, since there was no college "statute of limitations" that governed or curbed the period of time for imposing disciplinary sanctions.

After reviewing her experiences with Mr. Smith, I informed Ms. Barr that several instructors in another department were now grappling with a crisis involving his alleged disruptive behavior. I asked her if she would care to participate as a witness in the current investigation since there was no "statute of limitations" regarding prior incidents of disruption. In my view, if it could be reasonably demonstrated that Mr. Smith's current disruptive behavior was simply the tail end of a long skein of disruptive actions on the campus, this evidence would strengthen the college's authority to discipline him. Ms. Barr readily and generously agreed to serve as a witness, if necessary.

I then informed the chairperson of Ms. Barr's willingness to serve as a witness and he forwarded this information to the dean. A few days later he told me that the college attorney advised against this course of action since the student could not be punished for incidents that occurred two years before. I replied by stating that this was sheer nonsense since multiple, ongoing acts of disruption, no matter how ancient, constituted a pattern of misconduct and therefore were more serious and more punishable than a lesser number of disruptive acts. The chairperson pursued the matter with the dean and, ultimately, Ms. Barr was recruited as a perfectly acceptable witness.

By a strange and perhaps rather unfortunate coincidence, Mr. Smith at this time applied for psychological services at the Student Health Center and was assigned to see me. It was quickly evident that he knew nothing of my involvement as a consultant to those instructors who had filed complaints against him.

His own complaints related to severe anxiety and prolonged bouts of sleeplessness. His manner was highly suspicious and at times quite confrontational. With an air of considerable bellicosity, he insistently challenged my therapeutic style; specifically, he found it insulting and intolerable that I would want to know personal things about him but refused to disclose anything about my own personal life. This, of course, is not an uncommon complaint of psychotherapy clients, but I thought the arrogance and sense of self-entitlement with which this student expressed his demands were quite extraordinary and, if the truth be told, somewhat frightening. In other words, I was given a pretty fair exposure to the ill-tempered and bullying nastiness of the man, albeit on a smaller and more innocuous scale than the complainants had experienced as his instructors.

It made absolutely no sense for me to keep secret my role as a consultant to the college staff who had just leveled complaints against him. This information would only come to light later and Mr. Smith would then have quite legitimate reasons to consider me untrustworthy and duplicitous.

So, before he even had a chance to explain some of the possible causes of his psychological symptoms, I told Mr. Smith that I had already come to know him, indirectly, so to speak, as a result of complaints that I had received about his conduct. I was quite specific about my knowledge of his prior conduct, at the same time making it clear that, given my prior consultations with the faculty about him and my intentions to continue assisting those persons, I thought it very inadvisable for us to continue to work together. After all, I pointed out, I could not adequately assist his adversaries and, at the same time, effectively serve him as a therapist. Therefore, I advised him to seek therapy with someone else, perhaps off-campus.

Mr. Smith attempted to engage me in a dispute about the grievances he harbored toward various college personnel. When he asked my opinion about the rationales and justification for the complaints that had been filed against him, I told him without equivocation that, according to what I had already been told, he had seriously infracted the code of student conduct and stood a very good chance of being disciplined for his disruptive behavior.

I also made it clear that, as a consultant, I had no official authority to judge his case or to administer discipline. At the end of this interview, Mr. Smith said that he regarded me as a member of the enemy camp and therefore I could not be trusted. Apart from his usual predisposition to regard people with distrust and animosity, I thought that, considering my role as a consultant to his judicial adversaries, his judgment of me was quite valid.

A formal hearing was held. It was very long and very complicated. Mr. Smith contested each and every allegation and he evidently forced the judicial panel to allot him an inordinate amount of time to plead his case. The complainants requested that I be allowed to sit in on the proceedings in order to observe and monitor the process. Mr. Smith, without revealing that he knew me from our prior interview in the Student Health Center, objected to my presence, and, in deference to his objections, I was asked by the judicial officer to leave. Perhaps this was a wise choice by the judicial officer, since it removed at least one possible bone of contention that Mr. Smith could conceivable use later to discredit the judicial process.

Up to and throughout the course of the hearings, Mr. Smith had been temporarily suspended from Ms. Morse's class. In the end, his punishment was an indefinite suspension from that class and from the department in which the class was taught. I thought it a rather mild punishment for a person who had displayed a chronic and gross disrespect for the rights of college staff, brazenly flouted a disciplinary procedure (the formal removal from two consecutive classes), and threatened an instructor with bodily harm.

V. An Example of Reasonable Accommodation

Each day, usually around noontime, the sound of a high-pitched bark came crashing through the window of my office at the college student health service. Because the sound passed away quickly and the curtained window was to my back, I did not have time to turn around and divine its source. At first, forgetting that there was no driveway or parking lot outside the window, I thought this piercing blast of noise emanated from the burglar alarm system of a nearby car that had somehow been activated.

After a while, though, I merely accepted its regular intrusion into the quietude of my workaday world with philosophical indifference, although I never quite lost hope of discovering the culprit, human or technological, that produced such an odd din. I, of course, had no reason to expect that one day, in the not too distant future, the mystery of the disembodied bark would be solved with relative ease.

On that day I received a visit from an instructor in the engineering department who sought my advice about a student in one of his classes. The instructor stated that he had a problem with one of his students that he simply could not resolve. When I inquired about the nature of his concerns, the instructor hesitated and then a bit self-consciously stated that the problem was rather extraordinary, so perplexingly unusual that he did not know how to confront it.

With some prodding from me, he recounted how, since the inception of the semester, he had been unsuccessfully attempting to deal with one of his students who intermittently barked during the lectures and discussion that took place in his class. This student's barking was not frequent but its shrill, primitive and unheralded quality completely alarmed and unnerved his classmates and his instructor alike, who began to consider this behavior to be the first stage of some malignant and dangerous malady.

After receiving a fuller description of the student and ascertaining that he seemed to be rather normal in all other respects, I ventured a guess that the student's barking was one of the classic symptoms of a neurological condition known as *Gilles de la Tourette's*, which, as a form of tic, typically causes involuntary barking, motor incoordination, echolalia (the pathological repetition of what is said by other people) or coprolalia (the uncontrollable use of obscene language). Although I could not be absolutely positive that my diagnosis from afar was correct, I had read a bit about Tourette's Syndrome and was reasonably sure that the engineering student's symptoms conformed to this clinical picture.

I shared my speculation with the instructor and then devised a plan of action. I suggested that the instructor meet with the student in his private office, using the meeting as an opportunity to ascertain the underlying nature of the condition that caused his barking. He could, I suggested, let the student know that his barking was a distraction because it was both unexpected and unexplained. Perhaps the student could explain this behavior to the instructor who, in turn, could discuss it with the other students in the class, thereby alleviating some of the stigma and fear that presently surrounded his mysterious classroom conduct.

The instructor seemed pleased with these suggestions, and, emboldened by the possibility of resolving this problem without the use of disciplinary or punitive measures, he immediately formulated a plan to meet with the student at their earliest mutual convenience.

A few days later the instructor returned in a far better mood. With an obvious sense of relief and satisfaction, he related the following course of events. He met with the student in his private office. After explaining his concerns and expressing a wish to understand the true nature of the student's behavior, he was told by the student that the barking was indeed a symptom of Tourette's Syndrome, a condition that had afflicted him since early childhood.

When asked by the instructor if he, the instructor, could openly discuss the matter with the student's classmates in order to demystify and destigmatize his behavior, the student said that he considered it far preferable that he himself undertake this task, since he was not only a lifelong victim of the condition but was also a recognized authority on the subject, thus having a vantage point from which he could discuss the matter knowledgeably and objectively. The instructor readily and gladly gave the student permission to lead such a discussion at the very next class.

The student gave a brief but very edifying talk on the physical and social aspects of Tourette's Syndrome. His classmates were attentive and respectful throughout the talk and when it was over it was obvious that they had been emotionally moved, and apparently transformed, by what they had heard. Soon after the instructor resumed lecturing, the student emitted his intermittent yelps. No one seemed to pay particular attention and never again, at least in that class, was the student's barking considered strange or disruptive.

Soon after my second conference with the instructor, the student scheduled a session with me. He had learned from the instructor that I had interceded in his behalf and wanted to discuss the experience with me. The student was, as he himself claimed, an authority on the subject of Tourette's Syndrome. As a matter of fact, he was the current president of a local chapter of a Gilles de la Tourette's association.

While thanking me for my assistance, he also wanted me to know that he and his family were, in their view, done a terrible disservice by the psychiatric profession for many years.

As a small child, when he began to manifest the first signs of his neurological condition, he was taken to a psychoanalyst. The psychoanalyst was convinced that the condition was entirely psychogenic (originating in the mind) and that the child's symptoms were manifestations of emotional conflicts that were caused by family relationships. Without a medical examination or evaluation, a course of psychoanalysis was recommended and conducted for many years, a treatment that entailed a cost of many thousands of dollars and, in the end, availed no discernible benefit to the patient or his family. Out of justifiable disappointment and bitterness, his parents ended his psychoanalysis and consulted a neurologist. It was then that he was diagnosed as having Tourette's Syndrome and placed on a regimen of medications that have helped him ever since to control his symptoms and stabilize his life.

In the ensuing weeks and months after my single session with the student I thought of him often. I never saw him again but I now knew who and what it was that delivered the loud barking sounds outside my office window each day. Like the student's classmates, I could now—knowing their cause and source—accept these brief disturbances with relative equanimity.

Bibliography

Amada, G. (1983). Mental health consultation on the college campus. *Journal of American College Health*, 31(5), 222-223.

Amada, G. (1985). Organizing a community college mental health program. In G. Amada (Ed.), *Mental health on the community college campus* (pp. 1-11). Lanham, Md.: University Press of America.

Blain, G., & McArthur, C. (Eds.) (1961). *Emotional problems of the student*. New York: Appleton-Century-Crofts.

Boswinkel, J. (1986). The college resident assistant (RA) and the fine art of referral for psychotherapy. *Journal of College Student Psychotherapy* 1, (1), 53-62.

Brubacher, J., & Rudy, W. (1976). *Higher education in transition* (3rd. ed.) New York: Harper & Row.

Carmody, D. (1990, February 14) Colleges tightening discipline as disruptive behavior grows. *New York Times*, p. 7, Section B.

Close, C. & Merchat, M. (1982). *Emotionally disturbed students: Legal guidelines*. Sacramento, CA.: Chancellor's Office, California Community Colleges.

Ellman, R. (1988). *Oscar Wilde*. New York: Vintage Books.

Halleck, S. (1971). *The politics of therapy*. New York: Science House.

Koss, M., Gidycz, C. and Wisniewski, N. (1987). The scope of rape: Incidence and prevalence of sexual aggression and victimization in a national sample of higher education students. *Journal of Consulting and Clinical Psychology* 2, (2), 162-170.

Monahan, J. (1981). *Predicting violent behavior*. Beverly Hills: Sage.

Orleans, J. & Steimer, W. (1984, June 21). *Psychiatric withdrawals and readmissions*. Paper presented at the National Association of College and University Attorneys 24th Annual Conference.

Palmer, C. (1993). *Violent crimes and other forms of victimization in residence halls.* Asheville, N.C.: College Administration Publications, Inc.

Parrott, A. (1991). Institutional response: How can acquaintance rape be prevented? In A. Parrott & L. Bechhofer (Eds.), *Acquaintance rape: The hidden crime.* (pp. 355-367). New York: John Wiley & Sons, Inc.

Pavela, G. (1982-83). Therapeutic paternalism and the misuse of mandatory psychiatric withdrawals on campus. *Journal of College and University Law, 9*(2), 101-147.

Pavela, G. (1985). *The dismissal of students with mental disorders.* Asheville, N.C.: College Administration Publications, Inc.

Phillips, M., Wolf, A. & Coon, D. (1988). Psychiatry and the criminal justice system: Testing the myths. *American Journal of Psychiatry, 145,* 605-610.

Rickarn, R. (1989). Violence in Residence Halls: Campus domestic violence. In J. Sherrill & D. Siegel (Eds.), *Responding to violence on campus.* (pp. 29-40). San Francisco: Jossey-Bass.

Schachner, N. (1938). *The medieval universities.* New York: Barnes.

Smith, M. (1988). *Coping with crime on campus.* New York: Macmillan.

Smith, M. (1986). The ancestry of campus violence. In J. Sherrill & D. Siegel (Eds.), *Responding to violence on campus.* (pp. 5-15). San Francisco: Jossey-Bass.

Steadman, H. (1983). Predicting dangerousness among the mentally ill. *International Journal of Law and Psychiatry, 6,* 381-390.

Steele, B., Johnson, D. & Richard, S. (1984). Managing the judicial function in student affairs. *Journal of College Student Personnel, 25,* 337-342.

Steiner, C. (1986). Pursuit of knowledge or pursuit of suspects: Rights, legalities, liabilities. In J. Sherrill & D. Siegel (Eds.), *Responding to violence on campus.* (pp. 65- 75). San Francisco: Jossey-Bass.

Stoner, E. & Cerminara, K. (1990). Harnessing the spirit of insubordination: A model student disciplinary code. *Journal of college and university law, 17,* 89-121.